DU'

D

10

Purpose in a World of Chance

W. H. Thorpe

Purpose in a World of Chance

A Biologist's View

1478
1978

OXFORD UNIVERSITY PRESS
Oxford London New York

Oxford University Press, Walton Street, Oxford OX2 6DP

OXFORD LONDON GLASGOW
NEW YORK TORONTO MELBOURNE WELLINGTON
IBADAN NAIROBI DAR ES SALAAM CAPE TOWN
KUALA LUMPUR SINGAPORE JAKARTA HONG KONG TOKYO
DELHI BOMBAY CALCUTTA MADRAS KARACHI

British Library Cataloguing in Publication Data

Thorpe, William Homan
    Purpose in a World of Chance.
    1. Biology—Philosophy
    I. Title
    574′.01   QH331
    ISBN 0–19–217654–4

Printed in Great Britain by
Lowe & Brydone Printers Limited, Thetford, Norfolk

Preface

The relation between science and philosophy has always been curious and sometimes ambivalent. The links between observational and practical physical science (originally the sciences of astronomy, navigation, and mechanics) and philosophy (as the required logical basis of mathematics) have ever been close and cordial. For the esoteric and abstract activities of the mathematicians, though often seeming irrelevant to science, have never threatened collision with it and have often turned out to be of vital importance. Thus in 1645–60, when a group of 'experimental philosophers' were meeting in Oxford and London, a point was reached at which a design was discussed for the founding of a 'Colledge for the Promotion of Physico-Mathematicall, Experimentall Learning'. This led in 1662–3 to the foundation of 'The Royal Society of London for Improving Natural Knowledge'. It is clear, I think, that by this time suspicions were aroused in the minds of the twelve founders that too much theory (whether mathematical or not) might be a danger. So the motto *Nullius in Verba* was chosen to express their determination to withstand dogma and to verify all statements by an appeal to facts; in other words to prosecute 'natural philosophy', i.e. science.

Scientists at large have always held to a 'faith' that the basis of the natural world is rational and that evidences of some kind of basic design are there to be found. Without this the maintenance of the drive to prosecute pure science is inconceivable to many of us. A well-known expression of this is Einstein's blunt refusal to consider a particular theory of the universe with the words, 'God does not play at dice.' Einstein it was who also said (1938), 'Without the belief that it is possible to grasp the reality with our theoretical constructions, without the belief in the inner harmony of our world, there could be no science. This belief is and always will remain the fundamental motive for all scientific creation.'

It is, I believe, this conviction of the existence of some basic order which can at least be approached by the scientific method, that has curiously led to the present extreme lack of rapport between scientists and philosophers. Scientists could at least understand and appreciate the aim of the metaphysicians of the beginning of the century such as Bradley, Alexander, McTaggart, Broad, Stout, and Whitehead. But with the decline of the metaphysical school and its replacement by Logical Positivism the gulf widened greatly so far as many scientists, particularly those who held views akin to those of Einstein, were concerned—a group which included many biologists.

The widening of this gap was not, however, entirely a misfortune since it led some philosophers to leave the frigid, and in some respects sterile, heights and inaugurate what is something of a new subject, namely the 'Philosophy of Science'. The slow but steady growth of the new discipline, with its own journals and with new professorships appearing here and there, is a good augury for the future.

But apart from this, contact is now minimal; and few biologists today pause to consider current philosophy since it seems to hold so little for them. But when a savant such as Karl Popper, who has a profound comprehension of the fields of science, appears on the scene, then immediately the scientist becomes alert and eager to listen. And there is bitter irony in the fact that it was the Logical Positivists of the Vienna Circle, and their followers in this country, who largely ignored Popper's early work and who, whether intentionally or inadvertently, were partly responsible for the delay, of nearly thirty years, in publication of the English version of his great *Logik der Forschung*.

One of the reasons why I accepted my publishers' invitation to write this book is the occurrence in recent decades of two new advances in biology—each marked by a clutch of Nobel Prizes and each having immense philosophical implications. The first of these was the development of molecular biology, including the most important biological advance of the century and one of the most significant in its whole history, the 'cracking' of the genetic code. The second, more gradual and less spectacular, was the development of ethology to the point at which new insights into the behaviour of animals and the nature of the animal mind were achieved. So these two provide, so to speak, the foci of my book, which is in some degree both a condensation and an extension of my *Animal Nature and Human Nature* (1974). In more general terms it will also be a satisfaction to me if my book helps, in some small measure, to counteract a failing to which, so I feel, many scientists who write for the general public are prone—that is the perverse tendency to shock and disenchant rather than to synthesize and enlighten.

The death of two personal friends and colleagues of long standing, just as this book was nearing completion—Conrad Hal Waddington and Theodosius Dobzhansky—is a great sadness to me. Both of them readily agreed to my making a number of important quotations from their works and both had greatly influenced my thinking over the years. Waddington was an early colleague in the same laboratory; but our work then was dissimilar and we did not discuss philosophical matters—though we were already, and independently, embryonic Whiteheadians. Later we were in some disagreement—he being more enthusiastically a 'process philosopher' than I was. But finally his arguments prevailed and we came much closer in our views. Dobzhansky I did not get to know well until about fifteen years ago when his outstanding mental stature and sweet personality served greatly to enhance the already powerful influence of his writings.

Acknowledgements

I am greatly indebted to the following for advice and help.

Professor Mary Hesse, F.B.A., and Professor Dorothy Emmet between them read the whole of the first draft of the book.

For advice on physical and cosmological matters I resorted to Professor M. J. Rees, F.R.S., Professor A. Hewish, F.R.S., and Dr. William Saslaw.

To all these I wish to express sincere gratitude. They have certainly saved me from a number of errors; but none of them is in any way responsible for the views expressed, which are mine alone.

The figures have been redrawn with permission from the owners of the copyright as follows:

1 J. D. Bernal, *The Origin of Life*, Weidenfeld and Nicolson, and Thomas Y. Crowell Company, Inc.

2 From 'The Living Cell' by Jean Brachet. Copyright © 1961 by Scientific American, Inc. All rights reserved.

3 J. Lewis, *Beyond Chance and Necessity*, Garnstone Press.

4 P. R. Marler and William James Hamilton, *Mechanisms of Animal Behaviour* (after Wilson and Bossert), John Wiley & Sons, Ltd.

5 From K. von Frisch, *The Dancing Bees*, Methuen & Co. Ltd.

6 and 7 From *Animal Communication* edited by Thomas A. Sebeok. Copyright © 1968 by Indiana University Press, Bloomington, by permission of the publisher.

8, 9, and 13 J. C. Eccles in F. J. Ayala and T. Dobzhansky (eds.), *Studies in the Philosophy of Biology*, Macmillan, London and Basingstoke.

10 W. Penfield in J. C. Eccles (ed.), *Speech and Perception*, Pontificia Academia Scientiarum, The Vatican.

11 N. Geschwind and W. Letitsky from 'Human Brain: Left-hand Asymmetrics in Temporal Speech Region', *Science*, Vol. 161, pp. 186–187, Fig. 1, 10 May 1968. © 1968 by the American Association for the Advancement of Science.

12 J. C. Eccles, *Facing Reality*, English Universities Press.

Contents

x   *Contents*

List of Illustrations

TABLES

1
The world of matter

New ideas in science and philosophy
This little book owes its origin to the re-emergence of an old
controversy which raged during the first decades of the present
century and one might have thought would have been settled out
of hand. It has involved philosophers on one side and scientists
on the other. Fashions in philosophy come and go, each new
fashion no doubt resulting in the highlighting of some new
development, or some old development in a new guise, which
catches some people's imagination and seems in some way
to fit the problems of the times. But it is I think a fact that
really new ideas in philosophy or metaphysics are rare; so
that philosophy does not seem to us to make any steady
advance in the way that science advances. Indeed Whitehead
says somewhere that all modern philosophy can be looked
upon as a series of footnotes to Plato. Science on the other
hand—or at least the science of today—although it is no
doubt concerned with the same fundamental problems, seems
to bear remarkably little relationship to the science of two
hundred years ago. This is why we need continually to be
looking at old problems and controversies in the light of
new knowledge.

I must explain at the outset that I am a biologist who
believes emphatically that science not only leads to a better
understanding of the details of the natural world, but that
it can—a far bigger claim—yield some understanding, however dim, of the enduring reality underlying the transient
natural world. This amounts to saying that science is bound
up with metaphysics; and for a definition of that word I
think I cannot do better than adopt Whitehead's usage:
'Metaphysics is an endeavour to frame a coherent, logical,
necessary system of general ideas in terms of which every

element of our experience can be interpreted.' (*Process and Reality*, 1929.)[1]

The assertion that I have just made comes very close to implying that 'natural religion' is possible. Now it is true to say that there is today no general or widely accepted natural theology; and as a consequence many philosophers, theologians, and religious leaders have taken for granted that Christianity, like many other religions, is free to proceed and to recommend as divine revelation beliefs and formulations that owe nothing to science and that can have no relation to it. This is an attitude with which I profoundly disagree. I believe that the only possible basis for a reasonably grounded natural theology is what we call scientific. Here the difficulty is that there is no such actuality as 'science'; sciences are many and increasing in number. The pronouncements of these sciences are as yet very often mutually inconsistent. This is the root of our present difficulty in constructing a natural theology. Nevertheless, I cling to the hope and belief that a natural theology will in time become possible; and if in this book I can bring some gleam of unity where there was previously diversity and can take only one or two very small steps in the direction of reaching a metaphysic consistent with and linked to the basic formulations of science, it will not have been in vain.

This present work has been called into being largely because of the publication, seven years ago, of a book by the French molecular biologist Jacques Monod entitled in English *Chance and Necessity: An Essay on the Natural Philosophy of Modern Biology*. It will soon be apparent to the reader that the viewpoint I take differs very widely from that of Monod, and I feel that I and those who think likewise have the overwhelming mass of evidence on our side. Nevertheless it is a pleasure to acknowledge that both Monod and I avowedly set out guided by the same fundamental belief that to attempt to understand the natural world in the way in which science attempts the task is inherently worth doing. When we say that a task is worth doing,

---

1. The retreat of much modern philosophical thought from this position to a definitely anti-metaphysical stance is well shown by Wittgenstein's *caveat* that 'there may be no deep structure'. (See D. F. Pears (ed.), *The Nature of Metaphysics*, Macmillan, London, 1956, p. 120.) It is hardly too much to say that if scientists had taken such a view seriously, subatomic physics, at least, would have dwindled and died.

we mean that we believe that the results, if achieved by rigorous and cogent thought, will have their own intrinsic value for mankind. This 'value' implies what I call 'natural religion' or a 'metaphysic', though Monod would have used neither of these terms.

The old and the new physics

Usually science grows by small increments within the framework of accepted assumption, as happened throughout the nineteenth century. A then widely accepted view of science is neatly summed up in Paley's *Evidences*, which, until the second decade of the present century, was regarded by the authorities at Cambridge as required reading before membership of the University could be taken up. The main argument of the book was that if one were walking on a deserted shore of a new and supposedly uninhabited world and found, say, a watch or a clock, one would be forced to assume that the world must, at one time, have been inhabited by an intelligent being. The book emphasized throughout the clockwork-like or mechanical nature of much of the natural world, arguing from this that the world had been designed by a 'Creator'. The book was in fact the most widely known popular example of the 'Argument from Design'.

All this had arisen from Galileo's view of matter in motion, and its development into the mechanical or deterministic concept of nature held by Laplace. It was thus easy for the nineteenth-century scientist to hold the commonsense conviction that he was dealing with a real external world. At that time the physicist's conception of matter was of something composed of innumerable minute hard atoms something like billiard-balls, a conclusion which was regarded as beyond dispute. Thus what we may call 'naive realism' was supremely attractive. Many Victorian scientists were no doubt puzzled about the 'problem of knowledge'; but it was at least comforting that their studies seemed to reveal in a sub-microscopic world a landscape not different in kind from that perceived by the unaided sense-organs. From the material point of view the whole universe was a vast machine. But in 1897 the first crack appeared in this extraordinary edifice with the discovery, by J. J. Thomson, of the 'electron'. The world of science was never to be the same again.

These new ideas in physics were put before the world at large by two eminent astronomer-mathematicians in the 1920s, namely

Eddington and Jeans. Their writings made perfectly clear to all who wished to know that the substantial, tidy, materialist, comforting theories of the natural world had gone for ever, and with them had gone the rationality of making, in the imagination, concrete, physical 'models' as props and guides for theorizing about the ultimate nature of the universe. As Eddington (1929) said, physical science now turns its back on all such models, regarding them as a hindrance rather than a help in the search for the truth behind the phenomena.

We have the same desire as of old to get to the bottom of things; but the idea of what constitutes a scientific explanation has changed almost beyond recognition. And if today you ask a physicist what he has finally made out the electron to be, it will not be a description in terms of billiard balls or fly-wheels or anything concrete. He will point instead to a number of symbols and the mathematical equations which they satisfy. What do the symbols stand for? The reply is given that physics is indifferent to that: it has no means of probing beneath the symbolism. To understand the phenomena of the physical world it is necessary to know the equations which they obey but not the nature of that which is being symbolised.

And again, perhaps the most essential change was that it was no longer possible to harbour the view—or rather the disposition—which, as soon as it senses a piece of mechanism, exclaims, 'Here we are getting to bedrock, this is what things should resolve themselves into—"ultimate reality!"' Physics today is not likely to be attracted by an 'explanation' of this kind. Eddington stressed that perhaps the most essential change was that we are no longer tempted to condemn the spiritual aspects of our nature as illusory because of their lack of concreteness. Mankind had already in the 1920s travelled far from the standpoint which identifies the 'real' with the 'concrete'.

Scientific orthodoxy
One might indeed have thought that the writings of this period had clinched the matter beyond question. For physics this was approximately true. But for science as a whole it was certainly not so. Biology had until then been very largely imbued with vitalistic ideas, assuming that though the bodies of living things were undoubtedly material, there was animating, directing, and driving them some 'entelechy' or vital principle. But from the 1920s onwards, investigation into the physics, chemistry,

biochemistry, and microstructure of organisms was continually providing evidence for marvellously intricate microscopic or sub-microscopic mechanisms which seemed to hold out the prospect that living things would ultimately be shown to provide the outstanding examples of mechanism—even though mechanistic models and explanations had vanished entirely from the sub-microscopic world of physics. Slowly the old vitalist views were shaken or discredited. Thus it has come about that though the basic world of the physicist is even more mysterious and non-concrete than ever before, the world of living things has seemed (until very recently) more than ever a world of mechanical models, of chemical and physical models, of physical causality, and of mechanism. So it is that recently we have come to the point at which it is necessary to look once again at our knowledge of the animal world and particularly at our knowledge of the sense-organs, the brain, the mind, and the relation between these last two. But before we proceed to this it is worth noting a fact which is doubly curious: that there was a hangover from the nineteenth century of the philosophical doctrine known as 'positivism'. In spite of all that the physicists had been doing, this curious overall approach to the phenomena of the external world flourished and increased. Among its many tenets are the following:

1. That all which is known can be reduced to physical laws and that all genuinely existing phenomena have a physical foundation.

2. That the pursuit of knowledge can best be conducted when we limit ourselves to simple and relatively isolated systems.

3. That phenomena and processes which have a genuine existence are deterministic in nature or else (as in evolution) are a matter of pure chance.

4. That the behaviour or action of large and complex systems is the result of the behaviour of their constituent parts as they are to be understood when investigated separately and in isolation; so that the total behaviour equals the sum of its parts. (Skolimowski, 1974.)

So to all the central and profound problems of science the positivists had a simple solution. As Heisenberg (1971) puts it, 'To the positivists the world must be divided into that which we can say clearly and the rest, which we had better pass over in silence. But can anyone conceive of a more pointless philosophy, seeing that what we can say clearly amounts to next to nothing? If we omitted all that is unclear we would probably be left with completely uninteresting and trivial tautologies.'

Truly, scientific orthodoxies, like other orthodoxies, are sometimes very strange; and it is odd indeed that scientists are so susceptible to self-hypnotic indoctrination. As Orwell (1972) wrote in a passage which had been intended to be part of a preface to *Animal Farm* but which was suppressed and only published posthumously in *The Times Literary Supplement*:

At any given moment there is an orthodoxy, a body of ideas, which it is assumed that all right-thinking people will accept without question. It is not exactly forbidden to say this, that or the other, but it is 'not done' to say it, just as in mid-Victorian times it was 'not done' to mention trousers in the presence of a lady. Anyone who challenges the prevailing orthodoxy finds himself silenced with surprising effectiveness.

Subjectivity and objectivity

The change in the basic views of physicists, described above, provides a convenient starting-point at which to consider a problem which is bound to arise continually throughout this book—namely that of *subjectivity* and *objectivity*. What I am going to say here relies heavily on a valuable essay on the topic by David Bohm (1974).

The word 'subject' implies, of course, a person who thinks of himself as having the power to subject the world to some pattern of order and structure determined by himself. Young children obviously pass through such a stage, imagining a world in which everything is subjected to their heart's desire. But there comes a time when the magic world of childhood is shattered; with much shock and sadness they come to realize that in the real world things are not as they would wish. This is the beginning of the notion of objective reality.

At the same time as this realization comes to children they also begin to realize that there are some things they can change, even though the vast majority of the objects surrounding them are completely beyond their control. So as we grow into adulthood, we see ourselves as active subjects who, by the increasing percision of our thoughts and extent of our knowledge, can to a very large degree change things in a way to suit ourselves and our society—and so, through technology and art, come to be creative, expressing ourselves by the things we make and by the influence of our actions upon other people. So we find that 'objective reality', though ultimately inexorably encompassing our lives and ultimate fate, is not *entirely* independent of ourselves as subjects.

Yet we have come to see more and more, as the scientific vision of the universe has grown, that it is infinitely improbable that even the whole of humanity, even in indefinite aeons of time, could by taking thought have a significant influence on the cosmos. Dr. Bohm suggests that in this way people were led to the notion of God as being the creative source of both nature and man. In this view subjectivity, ultimately to our great comfort, dominates objectivity. We come to hold the view that the order, the form, the structure, and even the subsistence of nature are to be regarded as completely dependent on the creative thought and will of God.

Now as long as people, by and large, could accept this idea through their religious faith there was no need to worry about the 'problem of knowledge'. For ultimately all that exists was seen as being determined by the complete and perfect will of God, so man could see the reality of things only through a glass darkly by his imperfect and partial vision of God. Descartes, who was himself a man of religious faith, yet also deeply concerned about the problem of knowledge, proposed in his 'Dualism' a simple and concise view of the world. First there was *extended substance*, which subsisted essentially as matter moving mechanically in space and time. In addition to, and quite separate from, this there was *thinking substance*—essentially mind, but mind that was without extension, which moved in its own way in the activities of desiring, thinking, willing, and so forth. He regarded these two substances as absolutely different: neither could have any relation with the other or any effect upon it. The resulting difficulties he resolved acceptably to the thought of his time by bringing in God, who by being the creator of both substances was also able to be the ground of their mutual relationship.

Since Descartes' time, however, religion has been weakening. Particularly with the coming of the theory of evolution and increasing knowledge of the cosmos, men were able to think of the totality of the external world as self-existent and not needing God either for its creation or its maintenance. So scientists went on with the Cartesian philosophy, not noticing that without God the two substances fell apart and there was no possible or conceivable relationship between them. So it was that the Cartesian philosophers became utterly confused and posed insoluble questions concerning the nature of knowledge. For if mind is a thinking substance, possessing knowledge of matter, which is extended substance, then one has to explain how mind can know that with which it has by definition no relationship. In short the attempt to reduce everything to mechanism leads to such confusion that nobody can actually adhere to it in what he does, even though verbally he may give assent to such a view.

Monod's Chance and Necessity

If indeed everything is the result (as Monod tries to argue) of chance and necessity in the motion of the molecules out of which the world is completely constructed, it would follow that any one individual must in all respects be conditioned by the motion of the molecules out of which he is constituted. Similarly another individual who had opposite views would be made to develop and utter them only through chance and necessity similarly operating. The collision of views between these two individuals would then be nothing but the extension of the collision of the molecules out of which they were constituted. This would lead to an utter impasse, for the individual who claimed that all was mechanical would have to assert that his views were true while his opponent's views were false. But in that view of the universe there is no room for concepts such as 'truth' and 'falsity'. The holder of the mechanistic view would have to imply that the opponent who consistently failed to agree with him must somehow be deceiving himself. But, as Bohm argues, what can it mean for a machine to deceive itself? And what can it mean for one machine to say that it knows that it is functioning correctly to give the truth, while it knows that another machine of a similar nature functions falsely? In the last resort nobody can help but imply that he himself, at least in principle, can apprehend and communicate a truth and that therefore he is not merely confined to automatic and conditioned reactions to the stimuli he experiences.

There is a pleasing story about Archbishop William Temple, who was in discussion with an opponent who argued that the Archbishop's beliefs were determined by his early upbringing.

Temple said to him, 'You believe that what I believe is determined by my early upbringing. But I believe that you believe
that my beliefs are determined by my early upbringing, because
of your early upbringing.'

But to return to Monod. Although Monod tries to hold a
consistent Cartesian philosophy, he is nevertheless aware of the
fact that because he does not attempt to bring the idea of God
into his argument the two parts of his philosophy fail to hang
together. Lurking beneath the surface of his arguments there is
the realization of the insoluble problem which besets him, but he
cannot bring it to the surface and cope with it. What he does,
therefore, is to propose that objective scientific knowledge
should replace religion, not only as a source of knowledge of the
world, but also as a source of authority which determines the
whole of man's being, even his innermost feelings and aspira-
tions. He is of course perfectly aware of the changes brought
about in the physicist's view of the world by relativity and
quantum theory; and he is clear that no mechanical explanation
is available for the ultimate constitution of matter, animate or
inanimate, or for the cosmos as a whole. He must also know that,
according to the widely accepted views of cosmologists, in 'black
holes' there is a 'singularity' near which all customary notions of
causally ordered law break down. So we find ourselves, if we
follow Monod, in the extraordinary position in which physicists
are implying that, fundamentally and in its totality, inanimate
matter is not mechanical; whereas molecular biologists are saying that whenever matter is recognized as being alive, it is completely mechanical (that is, it is reducible to a rather superficial
nineteenth-century type of physical chemistry).

The growth of knowledge

Bohm issues a timely warning that molecular biologists should
consider the fact that, in the nineteenth century, physics
theories were far more comprehensively and accurately tested
than is possible for the current theories of molecular biology.
Despite this, classical physics was swept aside and overturned,
being retained only as a simplification and approximation valid
in a certain limited macroscopical domain.[1] It is not improbable

1. The position today can be roughly summed up as follows. The 'mechanical' concepts of 'force' (of which six different kinds are now recognized),
'mass', and 'energy' are still mathematically essential to the 'new physics';

that molecular biology, undoubtedly magnificent though its achievements are, will sooner or later undergo a similar fate. It is no use the molecular biologist holding firmly to a belief that what has been discovered will necessarily continue to work indefinitely, still less that it will ultimately cover the whole of reality. Such a belief must clearly interfere with objectivity, since it keeps the mind blinkered and unable to look in new directions which might give a vision of the dangers to come. This of course does not imply that molecular biologists should not press ahead with all their energies for the advancement of their chosen field; far from it! But it does provide a warning against using it alone as a broad basis for philosophical speculation. In short the mind must be eternally open, free of dogmatism, and ready to enquire in new ways and new directions. Bohm thus takes the view that the sharp division of subject and object has broken down; for the subject, which in principle includes the whole of society, can to some extent be treated as an object of knowledge. Thus the subject participates in an essential way in the object and in fact is an essential part or aspect of the object.

Knowledge is thus regarded as a movement or a process with two sides, subjective and objective. Any content that was on one side will be found in another stage on the other. While the two sides can be treated, for limited purposes, as separate, they both suggest and indicate one and the same total reality. There is no point in attempting to define the categories of subject and object once and for all. Such attempts are likely in the end to introduce unresolvable confusion.

Cosmology

We have witnessed lately, in the field of cosmology, examples of the 'growth of knowledge' of unparalleled significance in their effects on our view as to the nature of the cosmos—especially on the question of the primacy of mind in nature, discussed in Chapter 5 below. For modern cosmology has come to show that the universe is basically far more appropriate for the emergence of life than was previously suspected.

It is now generally accepted that our universe originated in a 'hot big bang' somewhere between ten and twenty thousand

---

While the word 'particle' is used to imply an object 'constructed' of pure 'energy'.

million years ago. But, far more than this, it now appears that
the essential nature and development of the universe must have
been determined (perhaps 'programmed' is not too strong
a word) during the first micro-seconds of this cataclysmic
event.

The first point which can be made with certainty is that if the
universe were not much as it is, neither ourselves nor other forms
of life could have come into existence. If (1) the universe were
not expanding, if (2) there were no stars, if (3) the proton-proton
force were slightly different—without (4) a certain ratio between
the basic forces of interaction and (5) a certain relationship
between the fundamental constants—without all the space and
time in the cosmos, the universe would be 'dead'. For even an
apparently trivial difference in any of these five features would
result in the 'evolution' and diversity of the cosmos being impossible to conceive. In particular, the present theory of the periodic
system explains the production of the heavier nuclei through the
fusion of several hydrogen nuclei. These heavier elements, such
as carbon and iron, are essential to life. All the evidence points
to the conclusion that it is only under the circumstances of intense gravitational contraction, which leads to supernovae ex-
plosions, that the heavier elements, necessary for biological
evolution to take place, can have been formed. And it is only as
another result of supernovae outbursts that these elements can
have been spewed out into space and so made available to stars
—including suns with solar systems such as ours.

So it is this chain of events which, during an estimated ten
or twenty thousand million years, has provided the infinitude
of time and space needed to allow the creation and death of
myriads of galaxies and stars, which in due course have provided
our planet with the heavy elements which render possible the
evolution of life and which we all, of necessity, carry around in
our bodies.

Thus it is the astounding coherence of the universe as a whole
which has determined that the present state of the cosmos should
have resulted from the initial events occurring in a minute fraction of a second at the commencement of the 'big bang'—the
very 'onset of time'.

Indeed one can say that the 'Argument from Design' has been
brought back to a central position in our thought, from which
it was banished by the theory of 'evolution by natural selection'

more than a century ago. There seems now to be justification for assuming that from its first moment the universe was 'ordered' or programmed—was in fact Cosmos, not Chaos. So, as will be argued later in the book, we have added reasons for considering the 'mental pole' as primary in Nature.

References to Chapter 1

Ayala, F. J., and Dobzhansky, T. (eds.) (1974) *Studies in the philosophy of biology*, Macmillan, London.

Bastin, T. (ed.) (1971) *Quantum theory and beyond*, Cambridge University Press, Cambridge and London.

Bohm, D. (1974) 'On the subjectivity and objectivity of knowledge', in Lewis (1974): see below.

Eddington, A. S. (1929) *Science and the unseen world* (Swarthmore Lecture), George Allen and Unwin, London.

Heisenberg, W. (1971) *Physics and beyond*, George Allen and Unwin, London. (See especially Ch. 17.)

Hesse, M. (1974) 'Worlds, selves and theories', *Cambridge Review* **95**, 62–5.

Lewis, J. (ed.) (1974) *Beyond chance and necessity*, Garnstone Press, London. (Paperback edn., Teilhard Centre for the Future of Man, London, 1976.)

Monod, J. (1971) *Chance and necessity*, Collins, London.

Paley, W. (1794) *A view of the evidences of Christianity*.

Pears, D. F. (ed.) (1956) *The nature of metaphysics*, Macmillan, London.

Skolimowski, H. (1974) 'Problems of rationality in biology', in Ayala and Dobzhansky (1974): see above.

Whitehead, A. N. (1929) *Process and reality: an essay in cosmology*, Cambridge University Press and Macmillan, New York.

2
Living mechanisms

The idea of a machine

In everyday language, when we speak of a machine we mean a physical system, put together by a designer or manufacturer in order to carry out certain predetermined procedures. Every machine, provided we exclude the very simplest (such as a lever or a hatchet, and those we can regard as 'tools' and refrain from dignifying with the name 'machine'), is made up of a number of parts, each of which has some particular function or functions in the operation of the whole machine and each of which stands in some definite relation to each of the other parts. This is true of the whole range of machines, from the most elementary (such as a bicycle, a coffee-grinder, or a clock) to the most elaborate (such as a television set or an advanced type of computer). All the parts of such machines can be said to be 'adaptive' in that they perform individual functions which contribute towards the performance of the machine as a whole. All these purposes and adaptations have been arranged by the designer; and we cannot understand or explain the machine until we know what it is 'for'. But once we know this, and have the specification of the machine, we can, by taking a certain amount of trouble, find a reason and function for every part.

In the time before mankind had passed the age of simple tool-making and reached the stage of constructing complex tools with component moving parts, we know of no objects in the inanimate universe which we could confidently describe as machine-like; for of nothing in the natural inanimate universe can we confidently ask the question 'What is this for?' and conceive of a reasonable answer. And this of course was precisely Paley's argument. One cannot sensibly ask of a glacier, a waterfall, a comet, a solar system, or a galaxy, 'What is this for?' unless the cosmologists dare to tell us that the super-novae are 'for' making heavy elements and so preparing the way for life!

Machine-like structures in living organisms

In striking contrast to all this, directly we come to examine the living world and begin to appreciate the form, function, organization, and structure of animals and plants, we find ourselves beset on every hand by machine-like objects. That is to say, living things have parts which stand in a relation of existential dependence to one another: for example, limbs, digestive systems, circulatory systems, and brains. The electron microscope reveals such machine-like structures, at the molecular level of organization, even in viruses (see Fig. 1). And in a single cell we find organelles, so to speak 'micro-organs', each of which seems to constitute some essential part of the cell's machinery for governing and maintaining what Sherrington called the cell's 'furious chemistry'. When we see a cell (Fig. 2 p. 16) in a diagram or photograph, we think of it structurally; but when a cell is seen alive, it is visibly a scene of intense and seemingly 'purposive' activity. To quote J. Lewis, 'The mitochondria are not static lumps but highly mobile; squirming worm-like back and forth across the cell spaces to where energy is needed. Everywhere there is movement, flow, change.' This in a single cell. The structure of an organism such as *Paramecium* or *Vorticella* (which, if not unicellular, are at least acellular) is even more diversified into functional organelles, 'still more vigorously engaged in perpetual movement, internal and external'. So we can ask of the structures in a living organism, just as we can ask of the parts of a man-made machine, 'What is this for?' and often we can at once give fairly exact and plausible answers.

Another distinction, of course, concerns reproduction. In non-living systems, such as thunderstorms or vortex rings, where new examples are generated, the new ones do not exactly reduplicate the old. Though crystals grow when in exactly the right chemical environment and in the right physical state, we should find it odd to use the word 'reproduction' of such substances. Living organisms reproduce themselves by reduplicating all the essential features of the design, but they are not exact molecular copies of the whole parental system.

Adaptive precision in animal systems and organs

So we see that the parts of organisms are functional and are interrelated, one with another, to form a system which works in a particular way or appears to be designed for a particular direction of activity. In other words the system is 'directive' or, if we like to use the word in a very wide sense, 'purposive'. And presently we shall come to another important difference—that organisms absorb and store information and change their behavi-

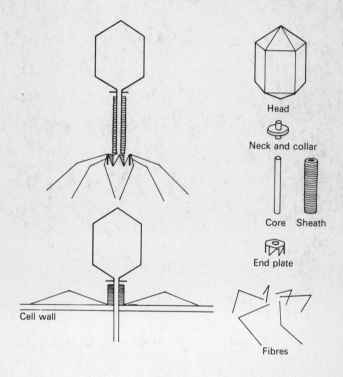

Fig. 1: A machine formed by a non-cellular living organism; a virus (bacteriophage T4) parasitic on bacteria. The organism is a sac about 1/10 000 mm long containing a reproductive substance, deoxyribo-nucleic acid, with access to a tube which is attached by specialized threads to the surface of the bacterium. The nucleic acid is forced through the tube into the body of the bacterium, where it multiplies at the expense of the bacterial substance. As contact with the surface of the bacterium is established the sheath shortens and the core passes through the bacterial wall, as seen in lower figure. Based on electron micrographs, magnification ×370 000. (From Bernal, 1967.)

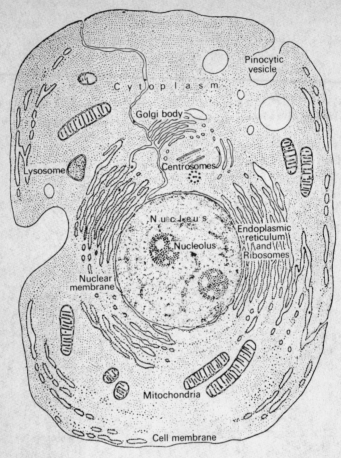

Fig. 2: Part of the elaborate machinery of a single cell. The diagram
shows the organelles which form essential parts of its machinery.
(From Pantin, 1968, after Brachet, 1961.)
Mitochondria: the sites of oxidative reactions, which provide the cell
with energy.
Ribosomes: the sites of protein synthesis. They are shown as dots
lining the *endoplasmic reticulum*.
Lysosomes: contain a whole range of hydrolytic digestive enzymes
which break down large molecules as required.
Golgi body: involved in the synthesis and storage of secreted products
such as glycoproteins and their 'packaging' within specially formed
membranes. (See also foot of page opposite.)

our as a result of that information. All but the very lowest forms of animals (and perhaps these too) have special organs for detecting, organizing, and sorting information, namely the sense-organs and specialized parts of the central nervous system.

It is perhaps difficult for the non-biologist to realize at first how overwhelmingly ubiquitous is this type of organization in the living world. In Fig. 2 we see a 'simple' cell with a number of its constituent or working parts. But every type of cell, in all tissues of plants and animals from algae to man, shows similar specialized mechanisms exquisitely adapted to their special functions. Should any of these types—be it liver, kidney, nervous, or secretory—fail to perform its function properly, the animal will, sooner or later, become handicapped to the point of death.

We can see the same staggering degree of organization in organs and tissues. The more we study, for instance, the sense-organs of even quite simple animals—the organs of vision, hearing, chemical senses (taste and smell), touch, position, and balance—we almost everywhere find steady and increasing perfection, yielding ever more precise efficiency in responding to the particular environmental needs of the animal. In spite of centuries of anatomical and medical investigation we do not yet completely understand the working of the human eye or the exact mechanism of the human ear. Still less do we understand the finest details of the senses of taste and smell. Yet in many respects the human mechanism is the best known of all.

The same overwhelming degree of adaptive precision is shown in the hard parts of insects, with their jointed limbs and hard external exoskeleton made up of a highly complex series of layers

---

Pinocytic vesicle: the first stage in the process of invagination, whereby particles of required materials can be taken in and held in channels and vesicles within the cell.

Nucleus: region of the cell containing the genetic material and the mechanisms essential for its division and distribution to the daughter-cells at the time of cell division.

Nucleolus: region of the nucleus which contains almost all the nuclear RNA.

The pair of *Centrosomes*, one shown in longitudinal section (as rods) and the other in cross section (as circles), which part to form the poles of an apparatus that separates two duplicate sets of chromosomes at cell division.

secreted by the dermis. Every student of elementary biology is shown at least some of these wonderful structures—such as the mouth-parts of the honey-bee, exquisitely adapted for probing into flowers and extracting the nectar, or those of thousands of species of flies, each species being able to suck, pierce, lick, or scratch to obtain the particular type of food for which it is specially adapted. Again, not only does the insect dermis produce all these astonishing structures, but the insect cuticle also is marvellously 'designed' to allow for moulting and renewal and to resist desiccation where such resistance is essential, as in a climate or micro-climate with the atmosphere at less than saturation; yet to be selectively permeable to water in certain aquatic insects where such permeability is required; and in short so as to adjust every single species to its proper environment.

Similarly, the feathers of birds show minute microscopical adaptations which govern heat conservation and allow every detail of plumage, colour (both pigments and interference colours), and form, to be produced. The feathers also provide for waterproofing and for adaptation to the exact type of flight—soaring, hovering, flapping, gliding, and every combination of these. It is probably not too bold to state that almost every one of the 6800-odd species of bird in the world could ultimately be found to possess special adaptations of feather and down appropriate to the particular ecological niche to which it has become adapted.

The same general story applies, of course, to chemical mechanisms within the body. Let us take one example: the present-day explanation of the breakdown of carbohydrates to release energy for vital processes within the organism. Fig. 3 shows the 'Krebs cycle' (a cycle, of course, in time, not in space) which allows for the breakdown of pyruvic acid to carbon dioxide and water, during which process its energy reserves are transferred to the ATP (Adenosine triphosphate) batteries. The pyruvic and similar acids all enter into the complex sequence of events which constitute the Krebs cycle, which begins and ends with oxaloacetic acid. The pyruvic acid is 'carried' round the cycle by the oxaloacetic acid and finally converted into carbon dioxide and water. Some of the steps are oxidations during which energy is transferred to ADD (Adenosine diphosphate). The last oxidation results in the formation of oxaloacetic acid, ready once again to carry pyruvic acid round the cycle. When oxidations occur they

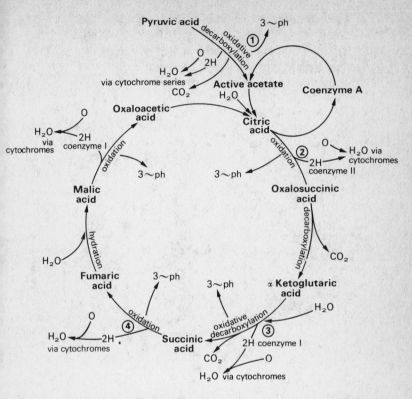

Fig. 3: One of the innumerable highly complicated 'chemical mechanisms' operating within cells and tissues. This shows the breakdown of pyruvic acid to carbon dioxide and water as part of the Krebs cycle. Each ~ph formed converts one molecule of ADP+ATP. (The symbol ~ph indicates 'energy-rich' phosphate.) (From Lewis, 1974.)

are brought about by the removal of hydrogen. The essential requirements for each successive oxidative stage are therefore the presence of the appropriate enzyme and of a hydrogen acceptor to receive the hydrogen. Thus the whole of this biological mechanism can be, and always is, explained and described in chemical terms. It is thus a chemical mechanism subserving the activities of the living organism which contains it.

Before leaving this subject let us return once more to insects with Fig. 4, which shows one example of the extraordinary chemical variety of secretions produced by the glands of ants.

In this case it is the 'alarm substances' which are produced primarily as means of communication between individuals, inducing an appropriate behavioural state (of readiness to respond to danger) in the ant which perceives the signal substance by means of its antennae or other organs of chemical sense.

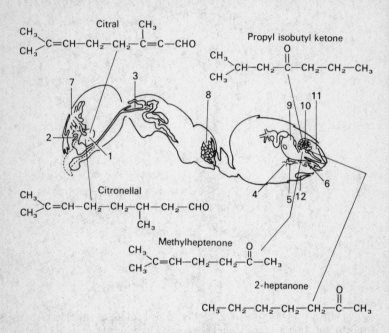

Fig. 4: Some ant alarm substances which have been identified and the location of the glands which secrete them. Citral identified from *Atta rubropilosa*, citronellal from *Acanthomyops clariger*, propyl isobutyl ketone from *Tapinoma nigerrimum*, methylheptenone in *Tapinoma* and other species, and 2-heptanone from *Iridomyrmex pruinosus*. The exocrine gland system represents *Iridomyrmex humilis*. (From Marler and Hamilton, 1966, after Wilson and Bossert, 1963, and Wilson, 1963b.)

The origin of animal mechanisms

When we come to consider the origin of animal mechanisms, we find ourselves up against the first of the two 'super-problems' which beset all who write and think in these fields These two problems are the Origin of Life and the Origin of Self-Conscious Mind.

In recent years there has been a spate of speculation about the possible origin of living matter from non-living. Many ingenious and not unreasonable hypotheses have been proposed to explain how the proteins and amino-acids, which are the main building blocks of living organisms, might have been formed on earth during its early history when water was condensing to make rivers and oceans, and when we might suppose that here and there rich solutions and suspensions of a variety of chemicals might have enabled interaction with sunlight to set in train, by lucky accident, the first steps leading to the birth of life. Many of these suggestions are plausible and indeed attractive; but even supposing them to be true, the 'life' that we can conceive of as being formed in this way could, it seems, have been only something of the general type which we can loosely call viruses.

Now, important though this could have been, it is of limited help in envisaging the origin of life as we now know it. The 'life' which might have been formed in this so-called 'primeval soup' has yet to be linked to life which reduplicates itself, leaving off-spring to carry on the race. The crux of the whole problem, as we understand it, is to envisage the origin of the cell; for all the life which we now study, from bacteria to man, is cellular in almost all its stages.

As we have already seen, the cell is a chemical 'laboratory' of immense complexity. The cell itself could not possibly function without the cell membranes which contain and selectively isolate the working parts of this laboratory. Biologists have long hoped to find a really 'primitive' cell illustrative of the stages between the supposed primitive acellular life and life as we know it now. But there seems little doubt today that there are no primitive cells living on the earth. All the cells that we know are of fantastic complexity. I believe that no biologist or physicist has yet been able to propose even the outlines of a theory as to how such a cell might have been 'evolved'. Monod himself sees that the evolution of even the simplest cell 'presents herculean problems'. The alleged 'simple cell' can be regarded as the paradigm or prototype of biological mechanisms.

Requirements for natural selection
In due course we shall consider natural selection as the driving force and filter of evolution, the creative principle which gives

rise to, maintains, and shapes the mechanisms which we have been considering. Natural selection can be regarded as a device for giving reality and persistence to new and possibly adaptive structures characteristic of organisms. Everyone knows that this action depends upon heredity on the one hand and variation on the other. If the offspring had no similarity to the previous generation, then obviously nothing could be conserved and chaos would result. Indeed, there could have been no continuing life under these circumstances. On the other hand, if every offspring were an exact copy of the parent, there could be no adaptive change (or indeed change of any kind), except that which takes place in the individual during its life. It is virtually certain, in this latter case, that life could never have reached its present lowest manifestations—let alone anything more complex. So for evolution by natural selection one must have offspring which are extremely similar to, but not absolutely identical with, the parent. That is to say that 'reproduction' must basically imply 'reduplication'. But no chick, puppy, or child grows up to be exactly like its parent. There are always differences between offspring and parent, which, if they are to be conserved by natural selection, must of course be in some degree hereditary or at least have a hereditary basis. This means that for natural selection to act there must be successive generations; and the qualities of the species and its individual varieties must be coded in the genetic mechanism so that, by a sequence of events, the coding of the initial configuration can lead to the adult individual. As Pantin (1968) points out, codes of this sort are possible in gross matter, as in the templates and moulds from which machine parts are reproduced according to human design. As all engineers and manufacturers realize only too vividly, however, even the hardest and most robust template or mould wears out.

For living beings the construction of a code capable of adaptation is impossible on the atomic level for two reasons: first, atoms cannot reproduce their like, and second, one cannot impress new features upon the individuality of atoms. There is only one level of material organization at which these two difficulties can be overcome, and that is the molecular level. Just by virtue of its atomic structure, a particular molecule can be repeated precisely (as it is in crystal growth), and, of course, it can be destroyed; but it cannot, in any ordinary sense of the term, be worn out. Moreover complex molecules, particularly if they are arranged in chains, can be constructed in sequences of more or less similar parts. Thus families of very closely related molecules, with closely related properties, can arise. The realization that the nucleic acids, with their chain structure, provide particularly good (indeed, one could almost say, uniquely good) possibilities for the development of very closely related molecules was the first major step in the great advance which resulted in the establishment of the genetic code. Further, it was found that in the nucleic acid family every molecule in the code of a cell is capable, under certain conditions, of reproduction by the construction of another code as a mould in a negative image of the first. From this 'template' the original can be reformed without any wear and tear. It follows from this that the code can be dynamically maintained. If a link be destroyed during the changes and chances of the violent metabolic activity which is continuing throughout every instant, without cessation, in living organisms, it can be replaced by a new and identical link.

The genetic code
This leads on to a topic of absolutely central importance, namely the storage and coding of information. Everyone today knows something about the immense development of macromolecular biology in recent years. It is concerned with the explanation and understanding of the storage and coding of information in simple organisms. Practically all the work in this field has been and is being done with simpler organisms, such as viruses and bacteria. Nevertheless there seems no doubt that this essential method of coding applies throughout all living organisms of which we have any experience. It does indeed provide a language of instruction for the development and growth of tissues. It lays down the essential blueprint of the organism in the sexual cells, so that the next generation of organisms is produced aright and is the correct copy of the parents.

Ultra-microscopic though the long molecules of DNA and RNA are, there is no doubt whatever that they are able to store a vast amount of information. I should like to quote again a simile which I have several times used (Pratt, J. R., in Kasha, M. & Pullman, B., 1962) which likens the information store in the DNA chains to instruction books which can be closed and put away, or opened and read out. Thus it has been suggested that a bacteriophage or virus, with a DNA chain, say, 200 000 bases long, has in its molecular instruction book 60 000 words, which would be roughly 300 pages of an instruction book written in English. The instruction book for a bacterium would be 10 to 100 times larger than this. And for man 'the genetic information in the forty-six chromosomes of each somatic cell is not so much a book as a very large encyclopaedia with forty-six volumes, and about six times 10^9 base pairs, two times 10^9 words and a million pages—an average of about 20 000 pages for each of the forty-six volumes!' And it must be remembered that such an instruction book does not of course specify the detailed positions, actions, and functions of the great hordes of molecules in each cell, still less answer any question of atomic species and activities. It presumably supplies the instructions for the structural and biochemical organization and functioning of the main types of cell. Yet we are still largely ignorant of the mechanisms which enable it to do even this. Truly we can say with the Psalmist, 'We are fearfully and wonderfully made.'

Programs and self-programming for development
When we understand the realities of this genetic code, we realize that the codes can be regarded as programs which can be stored in the living cell. These programs in fact amount to an internal self-representation or 'picture' of the structure of the cell itself and of all other types of cell which may come from it during the growth and differentiation of the organism of which it is a part. This concept of living organisms being uniquely different from non-living systems in having internal self-representation raises a point of profound importance.

In this book we shall later be discussing the other great biological conundrum, namely the origin of self-conscious mind or self-awareness; and we shall come to the conclusion that, as we proceed downwards from man through the animal series, the lower we go the less useful and helpful the concept of an 'experiencing self' becomes. When we reach the lowest animals the relevance of the idea of self-consciousness becomes vanishingly small. But if it be true that all living organisms have self-representation, does this not suggest the possibility that the first steps on which self-consciousness may ultimately come to be built occur in this self-representation and are present in all living creatures from the virus and the bacterium upwards? Thus it may be that the development of the very mechanism which is essential for reproduction was itself the basis for the later evolution of self-perception.

This development in the theory of the genetic code implies a biological discovery of immense importance: not only are the processes of life directed by programs, but also in some extraordinary way the living cell produces its own program. Professor Longuet-Higgins sums this up from the biological point of view by saying that it results in the biological concept of the program being something different from the purely physical idea of a program. He says, 'We can now point to an actual programme tape in the heart of the cell, namely the DNA molecule.' Even more remarkable is the fact that the programmed activity in living nature will not merely determine the way in which the organism reacts to its environment: it actually controls the structure of the organism, its replication, and the replication of the programmes themselves. And this is what we really mean when we say that life is not merely programmed activity but self-programmed activity.

Jacques Monod is as deeply impressed as any other molecular biologist by the appalling problem with which this confronts us in our attempt to account for the production of life (and in its turn, cellular life) from inanimate matter. This happening is now seen as so extremely improbable that its occurrence may indeed have been an unique event, an event of zero probability. Monod does, however, point out that the uniqueness of the genetic code is the presumed result of natural selection. Even if we assume this, the extraordinary problem still remains that the genetic code is without any biological function unless and until it is translated, that is unless it leads to the synthesis of the proteins whose structure is laid down by the codes. The machinery by which the cell (or at least the 'non-primitive 'cell, which is the only one we know) translates the codes, consists of at least fifty macro-molecular components which are themselves coded in DNA. Thus the code cannot be translated except by using certain products of its translation, the occurrence of which, in the right place and right time, seems overwhelmingly improbable. Sir Karl Popper (1974) comments, 'This constitutes a really baffling circle; a vicious circle, it seems, in any attempt to form a model or theory of the genesis of the code.'

In fact this undreamt-of breakthrough, far from solving the problem of the origin of life, has made it, in Popper's opinion, a

greater riddle than it was before. We may indeed be faced with
the possibility that the origin of life, like the origin of the universe, becomes an impenetrable barrier to science; a block which
resists all attempts to reduce biology to chemistry and to physics.
So unlikely does it now seem that the earth can have supplied
the necessary conditions for long enough to allow even a reasonable probability of the origin of life here, that Crick and Orgel
(1973) have been carefully and seriously considering the possibility that some simple form or forms of life may have been
deliberately transmitted to this planet by intelligent beings, if not
in this solar system, then in some other!

The very much abbreviated view of modern molecular biology
and the genetic code which I have given above may in some
degree be misleading. Like all other branches of biology it is
being developed and enlarged at a great pace. There have recently been published some important criticisms of some of the central tenets of molecular biology, but to discuss these here would
carry us too far from the programme of this book. Particularly
important are the criticisms by the molecular biologist R. E.
Monro (1974). As a result of a prolonged discussion with other
eminent molecular biologists and philosophers of science,
Monro comes to several important conclusions which can be
briefly listed here. He criticizes Monod for his excessive desire to
make universal principles out of the concepts of molecular biology instead of regarding them as part of a developing explanatory model. Munro makes three points. First, there is no logical
justification for supposing that the sequential information in
DNA is the *sole* bearer of hereditary information. Secondly,
there is no justification for supposing that the specific properties
of proteins are the sole means of expression of the information in
DNA. Nor, thirdly, is there justification for supposing that basic
interactions are all the same at different levels of integration.
Monro sees a distinct possibility that hereditary information in
higher organisms is carried not only in nucleic acids but also in
other informational structures or systems. And he points out
that micro-reductionist analysis should not be thought of as
excluding other forms of analysis completely. He then considers
the possibility of biological revolutions, which we have already
touched upon. Monro believes that the conservative attitudes
which Monod exemplifies predominate in periods of normal
science, and that only when serious anomalies arise and a

revolutionary situation is generated do scientists begin in earnest to explore their basic presuppositions.

At present molecular biology and related bio-sciences are still in a phase of rapid and successful expansion—normal science; but this does not mean to say that anomalies may not arise in the future. It cannot be over-emphasized that our ignorance of organisms is still vast compared with our knowledge of them. In the area of biogenesis, as of mental function, we have (as Monod himself admits) only the barest rudiments of comprehensive models. Monro adds, 'an essential characteristic of scientific research, in its more revolutionary aspect, is that the scientist is searching for the unknown; or, in other words, he does not know what he is searching for.' For an excellent elaboration of this idea from the historical point of view see Arthur Koestler's *The Sleepwalkers*.

The main point to bear in mind is that deep revolutions are still very likely to occur in biology and that such revolutions (when they come) may, indeed must, entail unforeseen changes in the way we look at organisms, including ourselves.

Natural selection: efficient cause of the production of mechanisms
Let us assume that life has reached the stage at which we have single-celled or multicellular organisms with sexual reproduction. How far, then, can we regard natural selection as a sufficient cause for the stupendous multiplication and diversification with which we are familiar? As we have seen, we also assume that living things are systems which have internal self-representation, and this in turn means that life is both programmed activity and self-programming activity. The result is that, provided there is some hereditary variation in the offspring and provided that the relation of these variations to the environment and its variations is such that some individuals have a better chance than others of living to the stage at which they can reproduce themselves, natural selection will ensure that those individuals or forms which leave more offspring will in due course become more abundant in the population.

Thus, the key point about natural selection is that those individuals which can survive well enough and long enough are enabled to produce more offspring like themselves. So we can say that those individuals are 'fitter' than the others and that natural selection ensures that it is the 'fittest' which survive. (Sometimes this comes near to uttering the tautology that it is the survivors which survived.) This means in its turn that those organisms which have better mechanisms for living and reproducing will appear to us, on careful study, to be more fully and precisely organized as 'machines'. It follows that, very widely throughout the living world, we see that mechanisms which appear to be better 'designed' have a better adaptive fit with the environment. So life is unique in being able to improve its programs.

But how far can this principle be the whole, or even the main, cause for the increasing diversification and adaptation, indeed the increasing growth of complexity, of which we feel convinced when we study the fossil record in the light of our understanding of the living world? It is of course quite obvious that new forms must constantly have arisen without the old forms having been superseded or eliminated. 'Primitive' animals and plants are still with us and the amoeba and the primitive algae are 'doing very nicely, thank you'. Indeed, there is convincing argument for saying that their existence is much more secure than that of any of the animals in the Red Data Book (the world list of species of animals in danger of extinction)—be they whales, Manchurian tigers, the duck-billed platypus, or even man himself.

Here we must take into account a fundamental difference between plants and animals. When we look as dispassionately as we can at the animal world, we can hardly fail to be convinced that there has, during the course of evolution, been a genuine increase in complexity of structure. In the plant world this is not nearly so evident; indeed, it is often not evident at all. Can we really say, for instance, that a pine-tree is less complex and efficient than a willow-tree? Can we aver that a fern is less complex, less well adapted to its environmental needs than is a thistle or a poppy? There often seems to be no real sense in which such questions can be answered in the affirmative. After all, the bracken, which is a fern, is one of the most wide-ranging plants on earth; and many species of fungi are so widespread as to be practically ubiquitous, at least in the climatic zone— whether it be tropical or temperate—to which they are adapted.

The limitation of randomness
There is a striking biological difference which, so it seems to me, gives a large part of the answer: plants are on the whole sedentary, while animals are mobile. Animals are in fact essentially

predatory-behaviour machines which have to go out to find and catch their food. Or at least they must be equipped with special devices (as with so many marine organisms) for filtering food out of the water, sweeping it towards themselves, and ingesting it in some form or another.

This emphasis on the importance of movement in animals is absolutely fundamental. Once an animal starts to move instead of being carried along by water or by wind, it has two choices. Either it can move in a random manner, in which case we must assume that the movement itself will bring it in contact with all that it needs (including food, oxygen, and water) and will ensure the normal development and survival of a sufficient proportion of the population. Or, if this kind of random movement is not enough, there must be directed movement; and of this there can be many different kinds. The first essential for the possibility of directed movement is that there must be some organs for detecting objects in the environment which can give guidance, either direct or indirect (e.g. by responding to the intensity or direction of radiation or gravity or to changes in temperature or chemical constitution). The more precise and elaborate the movements become, the greater will be the pressure to develop more precise sense-organs. Moreover, if an animal is going to move in a particular direction, it will be able to perform much better if it is elongate, perhaps to some extent streamlined. This implies that the most acute sense-organs, as well as the point at which the food is absorbed, will be at the front end; that is, the animal should have some kind of a 'head'. Even before this stage is reached, it is important for the animal that information collected about past events can be used as a guide to the course of events in the future. This amounts to saying that the sense-organs must be such that they provide for the animal 'rules' for its behaviour which must, on the whole, remain reliable, and not change abruptly and so make nonsense of past experience as a guide.

In Darwin's time and indeed until the rediscovery of the work of Mendel, it was generally assumed that acquired characters could be inherited; and if this was happening with sufficient constancy, there would be no crucial objections to the assumption that stocks improved and adapted themselves to new conditions by the ability to pass back into the germ cells the results of individual experiences during life. But the coming of Mendelism introduced the notion of separate hereditary factors or

genes; and linked with that, it showed the importance of study-
ing hereditary phenomena in crosses between individual organisms. And so it was, as Waddington pointed out, that those
students of heredity, such as Galton and Pearson, who confined
themselves primarily to the study of statistics about differences
and similarities between classes of related individuals—offspring
and parents, grandparents, first cousins, and so on—found their
work coming to be regarded as largely irrelevant. For the Mendelian doctrine implied that the only way of understanding these
discrete hereditary factors or genes was to study individuals and
the results of crossing them. The battle between these two sides
was a fierce one. Although Udny Yule demonstrated that the
statistical rules which had been adopted by the biometrical
school, whose chief leader was Pearson, could actually be de-
duced from the Mendelian laws if one supposed that complex
characters, such as body height, might be affected by many
Mendelian genes, instead of one or two, few were prepared to listen. So fierce was the controversy that this most significant result
of Yule's work was, for the time being, swept aside into oblivion.

The early Mendelians also laid stress on the importance of
mutation by which individual genes occasionally changed. As
luck would have it, one of the rediscoverers of Mendelism,
namely de Vries, had chosen as his experimental subject the
evening primrose (*Oenothera*). This was unfortunate because it
was found many years later that this genus has a most unusual
genetic system, involving an elaborate exchange of parts (a
crossover) between different chromosomes, and that de Vriess'
'mutations' were a very special phenomenon, depending on
recombination within the chromosomes themselves, rather than
on gene mutations proper. So it was that this work of de Vries',
led people to the assumption that such 'sports' or 'chance variations', which Darwin had invoked as the raw materials of evolution, provided evidence for the random mutation of genes. It
had long been argued by geneticists that the gene mutations were
random in respect of the immediate foreseeable requirements of
the stock. And this conclusion seemed indubitable when it was
considered that the gene was a highly complex molecule, held in
a given stable configuration only by quantum chemical forces
and liable to shift from one such position of stability to another as unpredictably and as non-deterministically as electrons
might behave in an atom.

The discovery of the genetic code has altered the picture. For now it is known that the gene consists of a string of nucleotides of which there are only four kinds, and that mutation consists in the removal of one or more bases from the string, or the insertion of one or more additional ones, or the substitution of one nucleotide in place of another at a given location. So we can see now that though these events may still be regarded as 'random', the limitations of the randomness are very much greater than they were before, since the events (which we can still call mutations) are dependent on the previous organizational history of the mechanism of the genetic code. Nevertheless it is still true that the alterations which such changes produce in a gene, and the effects which these alterations will have on the phenotype[1] of the individual which develops under its influence, are not causally connected with the natural selective forces which will determine its success or failure in producing offspring in the next generation (Waddington, 1974). It is regarded as abundantly clear that the sorts of environmental influences which affect natural selective pressures still have nothing to do with the induction of mutations appropriate to meet those pressures.

Since Mendel we have passed through three stages and are now in a fourth. To recapitulate: the first stage involved the concept of individual genes in the individual organism. This was superseded at the second stage by a view centred on populations rather than on individuals, but still dealing mainly with single identifiable genes. At the third stage came the work of Dobzhansky which taught us that evolution must be regarded in terms not merely of populations of organisms, but also of populations of genes. With this was associated the conclusion that the previous view (that in natural wild populations of animals and plants nearly all the individuals had essentially the same hereditary constitution, referred to as the 'wild type') was incorrect. Sewell Wright and Dobzhansky demonstrated together that in fact any individual in a population differs from every other in many genes. There is thus no such thing as a uniform wild type. In the fourth stage, we have come to think of the population as incorporating a pool of genes from which each individual draws its particular complement and returns it again to the pool when mating with another individual and producing offspring.

1. See fn., p. 32.

Natural selection: restraining chance and making evolution direc-
  tional

But then came another important development. Waddington
and his associates point out, I think with great cogency, that
natural selection does not operate directly on genotypes but instead on phenotypes, produced by epigenetic processes in which
the environment, as well as the phenotype, plays a part.[1] Now,
instead of discussing everything in terms of genes or genotypes
or gene pools, we have to look at the phenotype—where one can
no longer make the supposition that it is random in the same
sense as a gene mutation is random. In fact, as Waddington says,
if an antelope has to escape from a lion by running away, the
crucial point is not what genes it contains but how fast it can run
—which may or may not be closely determined by its genes.
When an unusual environment or circumstance succeeds in modifying the phenotype of an organism, the resulting modification
is, far more frequently than would be expected on a random
basis, of such a kind as to improve natural selective fitness.
Living organisms have a strong tendency to adapt to the environment they meet. As we shall see, this adaptation can often
be the basis of individual variation in behaviour, diet, free
choice, or preference for a particular niche (or for a particular
type of display), and these pressures do indeed often produce
alterations of the phenotype. Of course, there are many determining factors besides those that I have mentioned—climate,
soil, predatory species, parasitic species, and so on. In fact every
factor in an ecosystem can, at one time or another, have an
influence.

When we come to higher animals there is always the possibility that some members of the population may, as Waddington
suggests, decide to opt out and try something else. Thus the fact
that many island populations of birds fly less and less, may be
because, having given up migration, they have no particular need
to maintain their wings in the state of full flight fitness. (Indeed,

1. *Genotype:* The genetic information stored within the fertilized ovum and
   which can be passed on to the next generation.
   Phenotype: The manifestation of the genotype as seen in the mature
   living organism. The phenotype thus represents not only the effect of
   the genotype but also the direct effect of the environmental influences
   which the individual has encountered throughout its life and its own
   responses to those influences (i.e., epigenetic processes).

if on a small island you fly in a high wind, you may be blown away to sea.) Thus, Darwinian selection against unnecessary flight will tend to result in the elimination of those which indulge in it.

This provides a subtle system of feedbacks, in which the environmental factors which exert natural selection operate on phenotypes which they themselves have influenced in relevant ways (usually to improve their effectiveness), and in which the phenotypes in their turn have an influence on the nature of the selective pressures to which they will become subject. Chance is still important, but it is not important in the way and to the extent that Monod supposes in his book. The random nature of the processes which produce the elementary 'building blocks' comes to be unimportant when the building blocks are employed in statistically large aggregates. As Waddington says, 'As evolutionary theory moved into the orbit of Dobzhansky, Chance gradually lost the dominating position it had had for Bateson: and now . . . it plays an even more subordinate role.' In a similar way (as in the case of many higher animals) for creatures having the power to choose, experiment with, and learn about different environments, necessity need no longer be spelt with a capital N. Moreover the long-outmoded fallacy that random variations govern evolution has blinded people to the powers of selection exerted by the animal's own habits. As Dr. R. F. Ewer has said (1960), 'Behaviour is always a jump ahead of structure.' This is in fact what Baldwin and Lloyd Morgan said in *Nature* in 1897. But their suggestions went unheeded, perhaps largely because the rediscovery of Mendel's work, which came so soon afterwards, blinded people to the significance of their contribution and so it was eventually forgotten.

Another great advantage of this new way of looking at things is that the so-called inheritance of acquired characters, which is a completely unacceptable concept in terms of the earlier phases of evolutionary genetics, can now often be adequately simulated and explained as a result of epigenetic influence. In the first place, organisms usually react to abnormal environments in ways which are adaptive, that is, which increase their probability of leaving offspring. Secondly, there will be natural selection for those individuals which adapt most successfully. Thirdly, there will be some genetic component contributing to the appearance of the adaptive phenotypes. Waddington puts it as follows:

'Characters acquired by individuals are not inherited by their individual offspring. But characters acquired by populations are inherited by their offspring populations if they are adaptive.'

A penetrating assessment of these problems has been given by Thoday (1975). Dobzhansky (1974) comes to a very similar conclusion, for he recognizes that random processes are present in biological evolution particularly at the level of mutation and sexual recombination. Yet he says, 'Selection puts a restraint on chance and makes evolution directional. . . . Selection increases the adaptedness of the population to its environments. It is responsible for the internal teleology so strikingly apparent in all living things.' In evolution chance and necessity are not alternatives. In the evolution of man we can ask the question 'Was *Australopithecus* bound to evolve into *Homo erectus*, and this latter into *Homo sapiens*?' The question must be answered in the negative: 'We neither arose by accident nor were we predestined to arise.' But the behaviour of *H. erectus* no doubt played its part in the process of transformation into *H. sapiens*. Mutation, sexual recombination, natural selection, and in higher organisms 'free choice' are linked together in a system which makes biological evolution the only process apparently lacking foresight which is nevertheless creative. However, as Dobzhansky says, 'Evolutionary theory requires explanatory notions that play no role outside the biological realm.' I hope this will become abundantly clear in the next chapter.

References

Ayala, F. J., and Dobzhansky, T. (eds.) (1974) *Studies in the philosophy of biology*, Macmillan, London.

Baldwin, J. M. (1897) 'Organic selection', *Nature* **55**, 558.

Bernal, J. D. (1967) *The Origin of Life*, World Publishing Company and Weidenfeld and Nicolson, London.

Brachet, J. (1961) *The biological role of ribonucleic acids*, Elsevier, Amsterdam.

Crick, F. H. C., and Orgel, L. E. (1973) 'Directed Panspermia', *Icarus* **19**, 341–6.

Dobzhansky, T. (1974) 'Chance and creativity in evolution' in Ayala and Dobzhansky (1974): see above.

Ewer, R. F. (1960) 'Natural selection and neoteny', *Acta Biotheoretica* (Leiden) **13**, 161–84.

Koestler, A. (1959) *The sleepwalkers*, Hutchinson, London.

Lewis, J. (ed.) (1974) *Beyond chance and necessity*, Garnstone Press, London. (Paperback edn., Teilhard Centre for the Future of Man, London, 1976.)

Marler, P. R., and Hamilton, W. J. (1966) *Mechanisms of animal behaviour*, Wiley, Chichester.

Monro, R. E. (1974) 'Interpreting molecular biology' in Lewis (1974): see above.

Pantin, C. F. A. (1968) *The relation between the sciences* (edited with introduction and notes by A. M. Pantin and W. H. Thorpe), Cambridge University Press, Cambridge and London.

Popper, K. (1974) 'Scientific reduction and the essential incompleteness of all science' in Ayala and Dobzhansky (1974): see above.

Pratt, J. R. (1962) 'A "Book Model" of genetic information' in Kasha, M., and Pullman, B. (1962) *Horizons in biochemistry*, Academic Press, New York.

Thoday, J. M. (1975) 'Non-Darwinian "evolution" and biological progress', *Nature* **255**, 675–7.

Waddington, C. H. (1974) 'How much is evolution affected by chance and necessity?' in Lewis (1974): see above.

3
Life as purposive

The last chapter considered living organisms primarily as machines which have been made 'directive' through natural selection. It was not, of course, implied that these organisms are necessarily nothing but directive machines. Indeed, it was emphasized that the 'program tapes' in the cell sent out 'instructions' to the other parts of the cell, and so to the whole organism; and that life is unique in being able to improve its programs. Now we must consider what else there is besides programmed machines of marvellous ingenuity and complexity.

The appearance of purposiveness
It is quite obvious that many animals to a large extent (and almost all animals to some extent) show signs of what we can call 'purposive' behaviour. By 'purpose' we signify an intention to attain an end. But it must be made clear that the appearance of an intention to attain an end may often be illusory. Many animals are precisely programmed to carry out what are usually called 'instinctive' acts—such as the elaborate mating displays of many birds or the nest-building of birds and the nest-building and cocoon-making of many insects; and these often appear to show great persistence towards what we realize is the biological end of the behaviour. But experiment after experiment has shown that these examples of 'appetitive' behaviour, as it is usually called, are often seen not only to run off under inappropriate conditions but to be misdirected or not directed at all. In fact, far from the acts being intended to attain their natural ends, the animal often appears to be quite blind to these ends. There is no doubt whatever that in many species of birds, when the individual is constructing a nest for the first time, it may do so almost perfectly—yet quite obviously without

any understanding of the true goal of this behaviour: namely the hatching of eggs and the rearing of young.

If, however, we find that the animal is able to perform the approach to its goal under difficult circumstances by executing a series of original and appropriate strategies to achieve the immediate object, then we immediately get a much stronger impression of true purposiveness. This is shown clearly at a feeding table where the food is suspended on threads which are too fine for the bird to be able to cling to. In such cases some individuals of certain species (such as tits and crows) will learn to pull up the string or thread by a series of tugs, holding the loops of pulled-in thread with the feet. When this happens it can often be noted that this new behaviour is by no means stereotyped but that there are a number of variations in the pulling-up strategies so that the same overall action of securing the food is seldom accomplished in precisely the same way on different occasions.

This is the kind of behaviour which has often been described as 'insightful'; a great many examples are now known. A classic instance was described fifty or more years ago by Wolfgang Köhler during his experiments with chimpanzees in captivity. The experimental situation was a large and lofty chamber, the walls of which could not be climbed, and from the ceiling of which a bunch of ripe bananas was hung. The chimps would at first try to reach the fruit by standing on their hind legs and by jumping, but all to no purpose. They would then appear dejected for a while and make no further attempts. At the start of the experiment a number of stout boxes or packing-cases had been placed around the floor, and sooner or later it would be noticed that one or another of the apes would glance first at one of the boxes and then at the coveted bananas. This would quickly be followed by the ape dragging the box underneath the bananas and standing on it, only to find that this did not bring him nearly high enough. Then another box would be fetched and placed, often precariously, on the first, again without a successful result. Only when a rather tottery pile of three boxes had been constructed was the chimp able to climb up and quickly snatch the fruit before the pile collapsed.

The overwhelming impression on observing such behaviour is that the animal has worked out a new strategy in its mind, perhaps by a process of mental trial-and-error, and then put it into action—the whole performance being strongly suggestive of purpose. The above are some of the most striking examples which can be found. But hosts of other instances could be mentioned. For example, ants bringing back food to their nests, caddis-fly grubs constructing or repairing their cases, mud-dauber wasps carrying out repairs to their nests, etc., often give strong suggestions of activation by a true purpose—even though extremely short-term. Similar evidence could be adduced with regard to spiders capturing and dealing with their prey.

Methods of communication between animals: chemical, mechanical, visual, vocal

It is quite obvious that no animal could show this kind of behaviour in any convincing degree, unless it had already reached the stage in evolution at which it was equipped with elaborately constructed sense-organs. Without such, neither the objects concerned nor the possible ways of dealing with them could in any way be perceived. So we come to a characteristic of animals which has more than once been put forward as diagnostic—that animals are creatures capable of perception. By perception we do not of course mean the ability simply to respond to sense impression, but rather to correlate a variety of sense impressions into a totality, a perceptive world, however simple and incomplete. H. H. Price (1932) showed compellingly that, in human perception, the very idea of a material object is dependent upon an element of anticipation; and indeed that every perceptual act anticipates its own confirmation by subsequent acts. Another way of speaking of this is to say that an organism (even a simple and primitive one) in some sense searches for information and has some means of organizing and storing its perceptions.

Here again the concepts of information and communication become crucial to every aspect of the study of interactions between organisms. This is different from the concept of 'communication' used by many communication engineers, who employ it loosely to mean the transmission of information regardless of its origin or destination. They will happily speak of a rock or hillside as communicating with an observer if some light reflected from the rock reaches his eyes. Worse still, an engineer's definition of a communication channel does not even require a causal connection between the two points in question! Provided that the sequence of events at *a* shows some correlation with the sequence at *b*, some authors are ready to define a 'channel capacity' between *a* and *b*, regardless of the possibility that the correlation is due to a third common cause and not, after all, to any interaction. So in the engineer's sense, communication between *a* and *b* may imply (1) correlation between events at *a* and *b*; (2) causal interaction between *a* and *b*; (3) transmission of information between *a* and *b*, regardless of the presence of a sender or recipient; and/or, finally, (4) a transaction between organisms *a* and *b*. MacKay (in Hinde 1972) gives a delightful example. If we see a man walking in the street carrying advertisement placards such as 'sandwich boards', can we legitimately assume that he is communicating a message to all who see the sandwich boards? Surely not! The man may have his eyes on the ground and not see most of the people who look at the boards. Some people may be foreigners who cannot read the boards. The man himself may be unable to read!

On the other hand, most people, when they speak (or if they signal by Morse code), are directing their signals to some individual, known or unknown, in the expectation that communication will be established. It seems then that it is best to restrict the term communication to the sense in which a person or animal *a* communicates with a person or animal *b* only if *a*'s action is goal-directed towards *b*. By 'goal-directed' we here mean either programmed by heredity or experience to be appropriate to perception by *b* or to be emitted in order to affect *b* or individuals of a similar class or type. If this relationship between *a* and *b* does not exist then it is better simply to say that *b* perceives this or that about *a* or simply that information flows between *a* and *b*.

The vast majority of free-living animals have this ability to communicate information one to another; and the successful performance of this communication is vital to innumerable types of animal life of vastly differing structure and habits, from the relatively simple sea-anemones and worms up to and including the primates and man himself. All these communicate with one another concerning matters which are vital to their life and survival in a complex and hostile world. This amounts in fact to a study of various stages in the evolution of language. In one sense all such examples may be described as 'language'; and we do find it quite a difficult problem to decide in many cases where and in what sense we are justified in using the words 'language' and 'speech', but this need not worry us at the start.

Animal communication is of course of greatly varying kinds.

There is communication by contact, by gesture, by sound, and by odours and taste; that is to say, information received by the senses of touch, vision, hearing, and chemical senses. The last of these is the field in which knowledge is being most rapidly accumulated at the present time; yet since, compared with that of many animals, our own olfactory sense is so poorly developed, this is the type of communication which we find hardest to appreciate imaginatively. Since birds are primarily 'visual animals' whilst dogs are primarily 'olfactory animals', it is often easier for us to understand the behaviour of birds than it is that of 'man's best friend'. But the fact remains that although 'speech' may be reasonably regarded as the prerogative solely of man, 'language' is immensely widely spread in the animal kingdom. (For a fuller discussion of the relation between these two, see Hinde, 1972.)

Before coming to the higher levels of animal communication and to the speech of man, it will be desirable to examine very briefly the 'simple' and more 'primitive' examples of animal communication, to see how far, even there, we can detect traces of what appears, at least, to be purposive behaviour.

It is sensible to take chemical communication first because this must undoubtedly have antedated all other means of communication as they were developed during the course of evolution, though we are only just beginning to realize how pervasive and indeed how sophisticated it can be. Chemical communication is particularly achieved by the emission and dissemination of substances now called 'pheromones', which seem, in different ways, particularly well suited to communicatory functions. One of the reasons why chemical communication must have been primitive in evolution is that it can take place, with remarkable efficiency, in both plants and animals without the organism already being equipped with elaborate and specialized sense-organs for the receipt of the messages. As soon as there are cells which are capable of responding to a particular chemical substance, and particularly to changes in its concentration, the possibility of chemical communication is ready to hand. Also, it is not necessary, in the more primitive forms, that these substances be especially evolved for purposes of communication. And indeed, widely throughout the animal kingdom, we find that communication can be organized to a considerable degree by means of unspecialized excretory products.

A particularly striking example of chemical communication which has recently been analysed concerns organisms of extreme simplicity situated on the borderline between animals and plants, namely the Mycetozoa—or, when claimed by the botanist for his domain, Myxomycetes. In these 'slime-moulds', aggregation of wandering cells has to take place before the reproductive phase, which leads to the production of spores, can occur. Communication occurs by means of the discharge of a chemical called 'acrasin', which in fact may be more than one compound. This acrasin initiates the release by other cells nearby which encounter it (the cells incidentally being amoeboid in form at this stage) of more acrasin, and this sets up centrifugal wave-like pulses in the material. The substance not only induces acrasin discharge but also induces the amoebae to swarm towards the central producer. Although the acrasin has this extraordinarily stimulating effect on the amoeboid cells, it is also rapidly destroyed by enzymes which they produce. In this way a gradient is developed; it has, however, been shown that it is not so much the gradient itself that orients the cells, but rather the time sequence in which the relaying amoebae produce the acrasin. Thus, even at this extremely primitive level it is possible that the pulse-structure of the acrasin release may be the prime signal to which the animals are responding.

It seems that at an early stage in the development of chemical signalling, mechanical signalling was added to the repertoire. Again, this is reasonable because once two organisms are in close contact, such stimuli are likely to be perceptible without any particular development or specialization of the organs (which all animals must have) that indicate, to some extent, their position and movement.

The combination of chemical and mechanical signalling is beautifully shown in the spiders. Spiders are remarkable for their dependence for communication upon the vibrations conveyed through the threads of the web, combined with visual displays at close quarters; though no doubt there is a good deal of chemical communication taking place as well. Table 1 (p. 42) shows the generalized course of display in spiders—in this case not web-spinning forms, but the small 'jumping spiders' (Salticidae).

In the web-spinning spiders the male moves about until he accidentally touches the web of a female. From then on he is capable of detecting the species and sex (though generally not

Table 1
Generalized course of display in salticid spiders
(From Sebeok, 1968, after Crane, 1949.)

Male	Female
Becomes aware of female; starts display. Stage 1. (*Minimal releaser*: several sight factors; airborne chemical stimuli also involved.)	
	Retreats, or watches male, usually in braced, high position, often vibrating palps. Rarely attacks. (*Minimal releaser and director*: several sight factors.)
Approaches, in zigzags, or follows (if female retreats), continuing or resuming display. (*Minimal releaser and director*: above sight factors, plus type of female motion or lack of it.) Special female signs, such as vibrating palps and light abdominal spots, probably have directive value.	
	Becomes completely attentive; sometimes gives weak reciprocal display. (*Minimal releaser*: summative effect of display motions.)
Speeds up display tempo. (*Releasers and directors*: reduced motion of female, plus chemical stimuli. Self-stimulation is doubtless also a factor.)	
	Ceases motion, and usually crouches low, legs drawn in.
Enters stage 2. (*Releasers*: primarily, proximity of female; also involved, usually, her lack of motion, low position, and, doubtless, reinforced chemical stimuli.) Copulation follows unless female withdraws. *Director*: sometimes a pale abdominal crossbar.)	

the sexual readiness) of the female. In other cases the male may find the female by the scent of the drag-line which she lays down as she walks. Again, full copulatory behaviour depends on whether the female is in a web or not. If she is, the male generally uses vibrations of the web as signals. It may be taps or a plucking of the thread. If the female responds she may give aggressive signals, in which case the male departs. If she is mature and sexually ready, she may give signals of a different type, or remain passive; whereupon the male enters the web and is able to copulate. The predatory habits of the female when in the web make it obviously important that identification of species and of reproductive state should be rapid and unequivocal. Spiders, therefore, have a highly developed communication system using chemical, tactile, and visual clues (the last, however, being usually rather poorly developed).

When we come to the insects, we find an enormous development of the powers of communication. In the previous chapter a diagram indicated the chemical repertoire of ants (Fig. 4), and

Table 2

Ways in which chemical systems can be adjusted to enhance the specificity of signals or to increase the rate of information-transfer
(From Sebeok, 1968, after Wilson, 1968.)

1. Adjustment of fading time.
2. Expansion of the active space. Thus if the pheromone is carried downwind only a relatively small amount is required, since orientation can be achieved by the following insect zigzagging upwind and so keeping in the zone of stimulation—as do many male moths flying upwind, from truly astonishing distances, to find a single female ready for mating.
3. Temporal patterning of single pheromones.
4. Use of multiple exocrine glands.
5. Medleys of pheromones.
6. Change of meaning through context.
7. Variation in concentration and duration.
8. New meanings from combinations.

It is still largely guesswork which of these various categories are the more important, but it is certainly true that all are possible means of information transfer, not only in the Hymenoptera (ants, bees, wasps, etc.) but also widely throughout the insects and other invertebrates.

little more need be said about that group. But in many other groups of insects the enormous sensory development, associated with and rendered necessary by the great rapidity of movement, the powers of flight, and the highly developed social life— particularly in ants, bees, and wasps—needs further mention. In spite of all this, chemical communication has also been developed to heights not reached elsewhere in the invertebrate kingdom (Table 2).

In many respects the acme of communication in the invertebrates has been achieved by the honey-bee (*Apis mellifica*), and Fig. 5 indicates in highly simplified outline the chief modes of signalling in these most fascinating of creatures. This work is primarily that of Karl von Frisch and provided the main grounds for the award to him of the Nobel Prize in 1974. The complete 'waggle dance', shown in the figure, indicates both the direction and the distance of a food source. It constitutes for the colony of bees an extraordinarily efficient method of locating and harvesting, as rapidly as possible, a new and abundant source of food. The dance is performed only when a worker has discovered or is foraging at, a particularly rich source of supply. The dance on the comb results in a number of other bees setting out in the direction of the particular food source. If the source is still rich when the foragers reach it, they also dance on the combs on their return, and a numerous band of workers is quickly recruited to secure the rich supply. As soon as a source begins to fail, the returning workers cease to dance, although they themselves continue exploiting that source as long as an appreciable yield is obtained. The whole process serves not only to direct new foragers to food supplies which have been discovered by fellow members of the colony, but also to get them there in approximately the right numbers to exploit the food source properly without undue wastage of worker power. In Tab'e 4 (pp. 52–3) it is interesting to note that this communicative device is unique amongst the invertebrates in showing semanticity (item 7) and productivity (item 11) and is also unique in the animal kingdom below the primates in always showing displacement (item 10). Whether it really shows tradition (item 12) is doubtful.

No visitor to the tropics will be in doubt about the extent of auditory communication by insects—grasshoppers, crickets, cicadas, etc. The din in a tropical forest at certain times and seasons may indeed be almost overwhelming. Table 3 (p. 46)

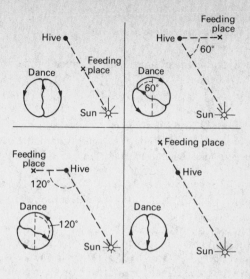

Fig. 5: The waggle dance of the honey-bee, performed on the vertical face of combs inside the dark hive. The direction of the waggle run across the diameter of the circle conveys the direction of the food discovery. In the hive the direction is relative to the vertical, in flight relative to the sun. Thus a following bee must transpose the angle of the dance to the vertical to an angle relative to the sun when it sets out to locate the discovery that the scout has announced. (From von Frisch, 1954.)

shows how these distracting medleys of sound can be understood and interpreted and indicates how the chirp patterns of different sub-families of crickets are designed so as to ensure that effort is not wasted when seeking contact with a mate and how cross-fertilization between species is reduced or eliminated. Figs. 6 and 7 (pp. 47–8) show the elaborate way in which the flash-patterns of fireflies are used to convey information for similar purposes.

Coming to the vertebrates we have to go a long way before we find any very significant advances over the invertebrates in regard to communication. The fishes have made an advance in that they have developed to an extraordinary degree their ability to recognize the differences between extremely dilute concentrations of natural food substances in the water; and there is no doubt that this kind of sensitivity is one of the factors

Table 3
The use of sounds for signalling by insects

The acoustic signals can be conveniently arranged under the following nine functional headings:

1. Disturbance and alarm signals (predatory repelling and conspecific alarming).
2. Calling signals (pair forming and aggregating).
3. Aggressive signals (rival separating and dominance establishing).
4. Courtship signals (insemination timing and insemination facili-tating).
5. Courtship interruption signals.
6. Copulatory signals (insemination facilitating and pair maintaining).
7. Postcopulatory or intercopulatory signals (pair maintaining).
8. Recognition signals (limited to subsocial and social species and functioning as pair- and family-maintaining stimuli).
9. Aggressive mimicry signals (prey attraction by production of pair-forming signals of prey species).

The use of the method is widespread, although the Orthoptera (including the grasshoppers and crickets) and the Hemiptera (including the cicadas) provide the major examples. (From Sebeok, 1968, after Alexander, 1967.)

---

which enable migrating fish, such as salmon, to return after perhaps two or three years at sea, with extraordinary accuracy, to the stream of their nativity, where they breed.

In addition to this, some fishes (notably the Mormyridae and the Gymnotidae, which inhabit the great turbid river-systems of Africa and South America respectively) have been uniquely successful in using electric pulses for orientation. They detect objects in the murky water by perceiving the electric-field distortion of the electric discharges which they themselves produce. It is also known that each species of Gymnotid fish has a characteristic resting pulse-pattern of electric discharge which may be modified by particular circumstances and activities. Among fish producing both strong and weak electric fields, casual observations suggest that the electric discharge may have a social function, though it remains to be seen whether such signals as have so far been described permit individual and species recognition; on general grounds, however, it seems highly probable.

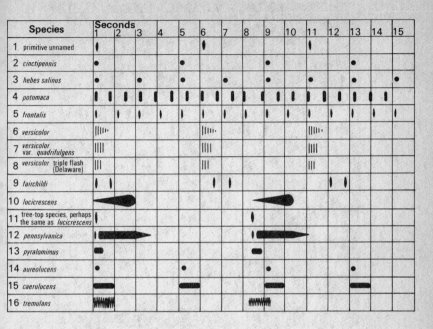

Fig. 6: Pulse-patterns during flashing in male fireflies of the genus *Photinus*. Species 2 and 14 (taken in Maryland and Minnesota respectively) have the same flash pattern but are quite different morphologically and may be allopatric (inhabiting different geographical areas). Delay times in female answers may be different between species. (From Sebeok, 1968, after Alexander, 1967.)

Bird voices

It is not until we come to the birds that we find features showing quite a close resemblance to human language and speech. The birds are (if we exclude the echo-location signals of bats and some other groups of animals) the most vocal animals apart from man. They use sounds to convey information between members of a pair, or a potential pair, between parent and young, between siblings, between members of the same species in a feeding, migrating, or roosting flock, and often between species within such a flock. Moreover, their vocalizations are incomparably more complex, more precisely modulated and controlled, than are those of most other animals. The apparatus for achieving these results, namely the syrinx, is unique in principle and in structural design.

Fig. 7: Pulse (flash)-patterns and flight during flashing in male fireflies of the genus *Photinus* as they would appear in a time-lapse
photograph. (Modified from Lloyd, 1966.) Small triangles near numbers designating species indicate direction of flight. The species
illustrated are not all sympatric (inhabiting the same geographical
area): (1) *consimilis* (slow pulse), (2) *brimleyi*, (3) *consimilis* (fast
pulse) and *carolinus*, (4) *collustrans*, (5) *marginellus*, (6) *consan-
guineus*, (7) *ignitus*, (8) *pyralis*, and (9) *granulatus*. (From Sebeok,
1968, after Alexander, 1967.)

It is convenient to divide birds' vocalizations into call-notes
and song. The former are usually simpler in acoustic structure,
consisting of one or a few bursts of sound, in contrast to the
longer and more complicated sequences of song. Call-notes, in
the main, convey information which may warn of danger, help
to control the movements of a flock, indicate the whereabouts of
food, and so forth. Song, on the other hand, is a type of vocaliza-

tion appropriate to, and often confined to, the breeding season. It is produced primarily by the male under the general physiological control of the sex hormones, and is often capable of a high degree of modification and development by imitative learning. Whilst the study of call-notes has revealed a number of features of great interest and has made it clear that they are very closely adapted to the particular needs of the species, the functions which they perform are not very dissimilar to those served by several of the insect vocalizations discussed above. Therefore we shall pass them over here and proceed directly to song.

Song is designed to serve both as a species signal and as an individual signal. There are some species of birds in which the pattern of the song appears fully coded genetically and almost, if not quite, resistant to exposure to the sounds of other members of the species or to other species of birds. It follows that the song of a song sparrow (*Melospiza melodia*), a wood pigeon (*Columba palumbus*), or a cuckoo (*Cuculus canorus*) is primarily, if not solely, an announcement that here is a male bird of the species in question, in control of a territory. In addition to this, the frequency of its performance may indicate to females of the species whether or not the owner already has a mate.

On the other hand (and this is a situation which seems to be far more usual), the song displays a good deal of variation in its fine detail which tends to make it unique to that one individual, so that such a song, whilst still being constant enough to serve as a 'signature tune' for the species, can also be recognized as characteristic of the particular individual. It is becoming increasingly clear that such individual differences can be recognized by mates, neighbours, and offspring, and that this is of great importance in the family life and social organization of a population. In recent years it has been found that this form of individual recognition is particularly significant in sea-birds such as guillemots (*Uria aalge*), terns (*Sterna* spp.), and gannets (*Sula bassana*). It is likely to be specially so in dense nesting colonies of sea birds because it ensures that the chicks, which are mobile early in life, seek food only when they hear the call which they recognize as coming from their own parents. A moment's thought will show that if this were not so, and if every hungry young one sought and begged food from every adult returning with food to the colony, chaos would ensue and a high mortality rate would eventuate (Thorpe, in Hinde, 1972).

  This type of explanation seems to be fully adequate to account for the development of the powers of highly refined auditory perception and the powers of vocal imitation, so widely found in birds. And in most species this imitative power is restricted to conspecifics, with the valuable kind of result just mentioned. As everyone knows, however, there are species such as the parrots (*Psittacidae*), the Indian hill mynah (*Eulabes religiosa*), and the mocking bird (*Mimus polyglottos*) which enrich their songs by borrowing from all and sundry in the neighbourhood, often solely from those of their own species, but sometimes, as in the last mentioned, from others too. In the parrots and in the Indian hill mynah this is not a normal feature of life in the wild but the result of the birds having been taken into captivity early in life so that, becoming attached to their human foster-parents and accepting them as members of their own species, they also take them as a model for imitation. But there are many other species which, like the mocking bird and the marsh warbler (*Acrocephalus palustris*), imitate enthusiastically any number of alien species which happen to share their environment in the wild. This may be a cheap way of acquiring individuality and variety in the normal song, for it is extremely unlikely that any two individuals will encounter exactly the same potential models in the same order and at the same period of their lives and so come up with identical songs. But surely, in such cases, song is less likely to be of value as a species signal, so its main importance is probably for individual recognition.

  It is not necessary to follow this subject further here except to point out the immense significance of the fact of imitation. It follows that a bird which is closely and accurately imitating another individual—that is, a bird which, by means of a long series of trials, is carefully modifying its own voice to copy that of an individual acquaintance—is doing something which powerfully suggests itself as evidence for true, though limited, purpose. It is hard to see how any simpler explanation could really suffice. For here we have the individual producing a novel and highly elaborate vocal pattern of changing pitches and timbres with a very exact and complex temporal organization. This is partly the reason why the songs of so many birds appear to us, and I think indeed are, 'musical'. This is particularly evident in those birds (such as the African shrikes of the genus *Laniarius*) in which the male and female together sing elaborate duets, which they work out between themselves so as to have a repertoire which is unique to that particular pair (Thorpe, 1972, 1973).

Finally, we may mention two other facts relating to bird song which seem to point very strongly to there being a purposive intent involved in their performance. The European blackbird (*Turdus merula*), whose song strikes the ordinary listener as being one of the most musical, has been very carefully studied over many years of recording and analysis by Joan Hall-Craggs (1962 and 1972). This work provides very convincing evidence that an individual progresses during the period of its song production and 'improves' both the form of the song and the relationships of the individual notes in a manner which conforms to human aesthetic ideals of balance and movement. She finds that if a blackbird is singing 'well' (from our aesthetic point of view) and a neighbouring blackbird approaches its territory as a potential rival, the singer may sing more vigorously, but certainly not more musically, in order to intimidate the intruder. In fact, on the contrary, it becomes a little upset and the song temporarily loose and disjointed; phrases are left unfinished, and pauses in between the phrases become even longer than normal. Thus it appears that the bird has to attend to the form of its song in order to be able to sing well by our standards.

If one records the song of a particular blackbird daily, throughout the singing season, changes of apparently aesthetic significance are detected. First, in the early part of the reproductive period, the song may appear highly functional; but later in the season, when the functional needs have been fulfilled, the song becomes organized more closely, and in a manner so nearly resembling our own ideas of musical form that it is difficult to deny that it is musically improved. So we appear to be moving towards the type which we call 'art music', where our experience of musical scores enables us to guess what kind of change is about to happen next. This sense of form seems to fit a number of bird songs in a most remarkable way.

Finally, in regard to vocal imitation, Brémond (1967) describes how a territorial singer, such as a robin (*Erithacus rubecula*), can sometimes quickly adapt to a rival by matching a section of its song pattern to that of the intruder. This instantaneous imitation of an invader's signal amounts to saying, 'I am talking to you, invader of the moment' (Busnel, 1968).

Purpose in a World of Chance

Table 4

*A comparison of the communication systems of animals and men
based on the design features of Hockett.*
(From Thorpe, 1972.)

Design features (all of which are found in verbal human language)	1 Human paralinguistics	2 Crickets, grasshoppers	3 Honey bee dancing	4 Doves
1. Vocal-auditory channel	Yes (in part)	Auditory but non-vocal	No	Yes
2. Broadcast transmission and directional reception	Yes	Yes	Yes	Yes
3. Rapid fading	Yes	Yes	?	Yes
4. Interchangeablity (adults can be both transmitters and receivers)	Largely Yes	Partial	Partial	Yes
5. Complete feedback ('speaker' able to perceive everything relevant to his signal production)	Partial	Yes	No?	Yes
6. Specialization (energy unimportant, trigger effect important)	Yes?	Yes?	?	Yes
7. Semanticity (association ties between signals and features in the world	Yes?	No?	Yes	Yes (in part)
8. Arbitrariness (symbols abstract)	In part	?	No	Yes
9. Discreteness (repertoire discrete not continuous)	Largely No	Yes	No	Yes
10. Displacement (can refer to things remote in time and space)	In part	—	Yes	No
11. Openness (new messages easily coined)	Yes	No	Yes	No
12. Tradition (conventions passed on by teaching and learning)	Yes	Yes?	No?	No
13. Duality of patterning (signal elements meaningless, pattern combinations meaningful)	No	?	No	No
14. Prevarication (ability to lie or talk nonsense)	Yes	No	No	No
15. Reflectiveness (ability to communicate about the system itself)	No	No	No	No
16. Learnability (speaker of one language learns another)	Yes	No (?)	No (?)	No

5 Buntings, finches, thrushes, crows, etc.	6 Mynah	7 Colony nesting sea birds	8 Primates (vocal)	9 Canidae non-vocal communica- tion	10 Primates— chimps, Washoe (non-vocal)
Yes	Yes	Yes	Yes	No	No
Yes	Yes	Yes	Yes	Partly Yes	Partly Yes
Yes	Yes	Yes	Yes	No	Yes
Partial (Yes if same sex)	Yes	Partial	Yes	Yes	Yes
Yes	Yes	Yes	Yes	No	Yes
Yes	Yes	Yes	Yes	Yes	Yes
Yes	Yes	Yes	Yes	Yes	Yes
Yes	Yes	Yes	Yes	No	Yes
Yes	Yes	Yes	Partial	Partial	Partial
Time No Space Yes	Time No Space Yes	No	Yes	No	Yes
Yes	Yes	No?	Partial	No?	Yes?
Yes	Yes	In part?	No?	?	Yes
Yes	Yes	No?	Yes	Yes	Yes
No	No (?)	No	No	Yes	Yes
No	No	No	No	No	No
Yes (in part)	Yes	No	No?	No	Yes

Animal linguistics

Table 4 illustrates a scheme, imperfect but probably the best available, for comparing the linguistic performances of animals and men. It comes primarily from the work of Hockett and Altmann. The first column on the left indicates the 'design features', all of which are to be found in human verbal language. The other columns deal with the communicative abilities, as compared with the peak example of man, of a number of different groups of animals.

In addition to this, it is to be noted that the columns numbered 1 and 10 refer to other aspects of human communication. The first is designated 'Human paralinguistics'. A word is necessary as to the meaning of 'paralinguistics'. Not all the sounds and features of sound produced by articulatory motions in the human being are part of language. As Hockett himself has pointed out (1960a, p. 393), the activity of speaking produces, besides visible gestures, a variety of sound effects which may perhaps be conveniently termed vocal gestures. Neither the visible signals, perceptible at a distance in the form of gestures or attitudes, nor the sounds which sometimes may accompany these are part of language itself in the true human sense. They are, rather, 'paralinguistic phenomena' and are of great importance when we consider the relationship between animal and human communication. For this reason I have included human paralinguistics in the first column. I have also used the term paralinguistics concerning columns 9 and 10, which refer to the social Canidae and to the primates. But in these two contexts I have, for convenience sake, omitted all consideration of vocal elements and so am speaking merely about the gestural or postural language of which these animals are capable. Column 10 thus includes the gestural ('deaf and dumb') language which the work of B. T. Gardner and R. A. Gardner (1971) and others has shown to be within the powers of chimpanzees when they are daily exposed to the use of these gestures by human associates. Chimps can learn to use it in the same way as deficient human beings rely on 'deaf-and-dumb language'—even, it now appears, to the extent of mastering the use of more than one hundred distinct words. This topic, of especial interest in relation to the distinction between animals and man, will be discussed more fully below.

Now let us consider, one by one, the design features themselves. It must be emphasized again that all these are shared by all human languages, but that each is lacking in one or another of the animal communication systems which have so far been studied.

1. Vocal-auditory channel. This design feature hardly needs comment. It has two supremely important characteristics: first, the production of sound requires very little physical energy; and second, in contrast to gestural communication, it leaves much of the body free for other activities that can then be carried on at the same time.

2. Broadcast transmission and directional reception. This and design feature (3) are the almost inevitable result of the physics of sound. Nevertheless, they are so obvious that they can easily be overlooked, and their significance and the benefits derived from them underestimated. Broadcast transmission is, of course, inevitable with sound, but directional reception depends upon the structure and design of the auditory organ, which, generally in animals and obviously in mammals and birds, is clearly an adaptive result of evolutionary development.

3. Rapid fading. This indicates that the message does not linger for reception at the recipient's convenience, but quickly vanishes, leaving the communication system free for further messages. This is obviously in strong contrast to such examples as animal tracks, spoors, and also the production of messages by means of those scent glands which secrete persistent chemical substances; likewise urine and excreta, which may persist for a very long while.

4. Interchangeability. This is meant to imply that the adult members of any speech community are interchangeably transmitters and receivers of linguistic signals.

5. Complete feedback. This simply means that the speaker hears everything relevant in what he himself says. The significance of features 4 and 5 for language becomes clear when we compare them with other systems. In general, a speaker of a language can reproduce any linguistic message he can understand; whereas the mating displays of, for instance, the spiders are usually confined to the male sex only and cannot be executed by the female who receives them. The same lack of interchangeability is often characteristic of those vocal displays which are known generally as 'song', female song being the exception rather than the rule in the birds. In contrast, however, directly we come to the 'call notes' of birds (which are used for maintaining contact and co-ordinating movements amongst flocks

and families not in breeding condition), we see that these signals may be interchangeable in Hockett's sense.

The term 'complete feedback' emphasized the important fact that we ourselves and, presumably, most animals can hear ourselves as others hear us but cannot see ourselves as others see us. This is a feature of communication systems of great importance in the study of behaviour.

6. Specialization. Specialization implies that the direct energy consequences of linguistic signals are biologically unimportant; only the triggering consequences are significant.

7. Semanticity. This refers to the fact that the role of linguistic signals in man is to correlate and organize the life of a community. They can do this because there are associative ties between signal elements and features in the outside world. That is to say, some linguistic forms have denotations. A good many anthropological theorists speak as if they believe that only human communicative systems are semantic. A glance at the columns in Table 4 will show how unjustified such an assumption is.

8. Arbitrariness. This simply refers to the fact that the symbols are abstract in the sense that the relation between a meaningful element in a language and its denotation is independent of any physical or geometrical resemblance between the two. For instance, the word 'square' is not rectangular, nor is the word 'green' coloured.

9. Discreteness. This implies that the repertoire is discrete, not continuous, and that the possible messages in any language constitute a discrete repertoire rather than a continuous one. This distinction between discrete units and graded units can also be regarded as the difference between digital and analog communication. True language is characterized by its digital information coding system. Thus we may have two words which are acoustically very similar but with entirely different meanings and with no possibility of bridging the gap; for example, the difference between the English words 'track' and 'crack' is discontinuous. If, by contrast, we look at the facial displays or the gestures of human beings and a great many animals, there is a continuum of gradations possible between the two. And although the two ends of the continuum may involve a change of message in between, the cues by which we decide what is meant are not discrete but are graded—the information coding is analog.

10. Displacement. Displacement merely implies that signals

can refer to things remote in time and space. Human language can refer to events millions of light years distant and aeons removed in time. They can also refer to events here and now taking place in our heads. Here, the difference between human and animal languages is far from concrete and very often may be merely a matter of the length of the time or space gap to be bridged.

11. Openness. Openness implies that new linguistic messages are coined freely and easily and, in context, can be immediately understood. Obviously, human communication is open; we can talk about things never talked about before. But so can a bee by means of its dances, since a worker may report a location which has never been reported before. Some bird-song systems are open in the same sense.

12. Tradition. This indicates that conventions can be passed on, by teaching and learning, from one group or generation to another.

13. Duality of patterning. This essentially implies that though the signal elements themselves may be meaningless, patterned combinations of them are meaningful. This is a feature of the sounds of some birds and also of the paralinguistic communications of animals such as the Canidae and the primates.

Item 13 completes the design features originally elaborated by Hockett in his papers in the early 1960s. However, Hockett and Altmann (1968) have since given three more which are numbers 14–16 in our table.

14. Prevarication. This connotes the ability to lie or talk nonsense with deliberate intent. It is highly characteristic of the human species and found hardly at all in animals. Possible exceptions occur in the play of some mammals and a few birds, where we see what appear to be gestures, feints, and ruses designed to mislead.

15. Reflectiveness. Reflectiveness, or reflexiveness, simply indicates the ability to communicate about the communication system itself. This is undoubtedly peculiar to human speech and not found anywhere else, as far as we know, in the animal kingdom.

16. Learnability. This implies that the speaker of one language can learn another. This is most obviously true for human beings, for there is no known human language which cannot be learnt by all normal members of the human race. It is much

more difficult to decide how to evaluate this in animals. Certainly, animals can learn new signals and the meaning of new signals; and learning plays a vital part in many communicative systems of birds and mammals. In birds, of course, 'imitativeness', i.e. the ability and tendency to imitate the sounds produced by associates of the same species (or foster-parents, as in mynahs) without specific reward, is an outstandingly important feature. Thus it will be seen that we can give a fairly confident 'yes' to this question in columns 1, 2, 5, 6, and 10, and a rather less confident 'no' in some of the other columns.

'Speech' by Chimpanzees

Having described and discussed the system of 'design features' elaborated by Hockett and Altmann, we shall now consider recent studies on the training of chimpanzees to 'talk', in relation to column 10 of the table. There have been, in the past, several attempts to train chimpanzees to use human language. It is not putting it too strongly to say that they have been monumental failures. The best-known was that of Hayes and Hayes (1952, 1955) with the young chimpanzee 'Viki'. The prolonged and painstaking work of six years resulted in Viki having learned only four sounds that approximated to English words and even then the approximation was somewhat tenuous. As Gardner and Gardner (1969) point out, human speech sounds are unsuitable as a medium for communication for the chimpanzee, whose vocal apparatus and vocal behaviour are different from ours. These animals do make many different sounds, but generally vocalization occurs in situations of high excitement and tends to be specific to the exciting situation. Undisturbed chimpanzees are usually rather silent when in captivity. It is consequently improbable that a chimpanzee could be trained to make refined use of its vocalizations.

With this problem in mind, the Gardners adopted an infant female chimpanzee at an age between eight and fourteen months and proceeded to attempt to teach this animal a gesture language known as the American Sign Language (ASL). This is the language widely used in the United States for communication between deaf human beings, and it is systematically taught to deaf children. It is entirely different from the deaf-and-dumb language of Great Britain, which essentially is a method of spelling—an alphabetical means of communication. Such systems of finger spelling are of course widely used by the deaf and dumb in conjunction with, and to supplement, sign languages.

ASL is composed of manually produced visual symbols, called signs, which 'are strictly analogous to words as used in spoken languages' (Gardner and Gardner, 1971). The Gardners point out that as words can be analysed into phonemes, so signs can be analysed into what have been called 'cheremes' by Stokoe. A system of 55 cheremes has been devised for ASL. Of these, 19 identify the configuration of the hand or hands making the sign, 12 the place where the sign is made, and 24 the action of the hand or hands. Thus the configuration of pointing the hand yields one sign when near the forehead, another near the cheek, another near the chin, yet another near the shoulder, and so forth. At any given place the pointing-hand signal yields one sign if moved towards the signer, another if moved away; another if moved vertically, and yet another if moved horizontally, and so on. But if the 'tapered hand signal' is used, instead of the pointing hand, a whole new family of signs is generated.

This summary shows that ASL satisfies the criteria for design feature 13 (p. 52), in that there are arbitrary, but stable, meaningless signal elements and that these are arranged in a series of patterns which constitute minimum meaningful combinations of those elements. The formal analysis of the ASL language by linguists is still in a relatively elementary state. But it is already clear that ASL has a syntactical structure of its own that is different from English. It will surprise non-linguists to learn that the complete linguistic analysis of spoken English is even yet incomplete; so, as the Gardners point out, it will be a long time before a precise comparison of ASL with English, in regard to syntax, can be established. But while such precise comparison is not yet possible, it is nevertheless clear that ASL is a language in essentially the same sense that English is a language, and that if a chimpanzee can be taught ASL to such a degree that it can carry on some or most of the normal communicative activities of its life by that means, then that chimpanzee has learned a language. The process of teaching ASL to a chimpanzee has the further very great advantage that the animal's achievements can be compared directly with the achievements of normal young children in their acquisition of English and with deaf children of the same ages in their acquisition of ASL.

The basic situation employed was as follows. A young female

chimp (named Washoe) was kept in a room that contained most of the usual items of a modern human dwelling. The environment was as interesting as possible, and the training programme was made an integral part of this environment throughout the waking hours of the ape. There was, however, no attempt to make the chimpanzee a normal member of a human family. The work was planned so that during the whole of her waking hours Washoe was in the presence of one or more human companions with whom she took part in the routine activities of the day—feeding, bathing, dressing, etc.—and with whom she played games, examined new objects, was shown picture books and magazines, and so on. However, the only form of verbal communication that was used in Washoe's presence was ASL; all her human companions had to master ASL sufficiently well for them not to need to use any other form of communication, with the exception of finger spelling for, unusual or technical words. But apart from the prohibition on the use of spoken language, there was no rule of silence. Vocalization was permitted if it was not verbal or if the sounds were sounds that Washoe could imitate, such as laughter and cries of pleasure and displeasure. Washoe's attention was obtained by clapping the hands and many other noises, and there was also music. Burglar alarms and boat horns were used to frighten Washoe away from forbidden places. After the first thirty-nine months of this work the results were as briefly summarized below.

One of the most widespread hypotheses initially invoked to explain the development of language in the human infant may be called, for convenience, the 'babbling hypothesis'. This assumes that the 'random' babbling and jabbering of the human baby comprises a great variety of sounds and so will include most if not all of the sounds which are employed in the language of whatever culture it happens to be reared in. Mothers often talk or croon to their children when attending to them, and so the sound of the mother's voice will become associated with comfort-giving measures. From this it is to be expected that when the child, alone and uncomfortable, hears its own voice, this will likewise have a consoling, comforting effect. So it is supposed (by, for example, Mowrer, 1950) that the infant will be rewarded for its first babbling and jabbering without any necessary reference to the effects produced upon others. Before long, however, the infant will learn that if it succeeds in making the kind of sound its mother makes, it will get more interest, affection, and attention in return; so the stage is set for the learning of language. There are, in fact, a good many difficulties in the way of this theory. Perhaps the major one of these is the difficulty, if not impossibility, of characterizing the kind of rewarding or 'reinforcing' event which could account adequately for the acquisition of language in such a learning situation. In fact, as will be made clear later, Chomsky (1957) has shown, with seemingly incontrovertible argument, that such a theory cannot possibly account for the basic events in the child's acquisition of language.

Nevertheless, at the commencement of the work with Washoe it was assumed that the infant chimpanzee would in fact show a great deal of 'manual babbling' in the form of random or accidental gestures, which would come so close to the cheremes of ASL that they could be readily enhanced and 'shaped' by the methods planned for the experiment. However, during the earliest months of the project the amount of manual babbling was very small. The ape would manipulate objects, poke at them with her fingers, and so forth, but she seldom engaged in the kind of manual play that had been expected, such as wiggling her fingers before her eyes or poking the fingers of one hand at the other hand. As time went on, cheremic and incipiently cheremic gestures seemed to increase in frequency, and during this period the ape acquired several signs which she could use appropriately. Moreover, she seemed to be paying more and more attention to the signs made by her human companions and showed that she could comprehend the meaning of many of these signs. Manual babbling was encouraged by the experimenters as much as possible, and one sign which did appear to be learned largely in this way was the ASL 'word' for funny. Washoe was fond of touching her nose or her friends' noses with her index finger, and in the 'funny' sign the extended index and second fingers are brushed against the sides of the nose. Washoe herself introduced a variation which consisted of snorting as the nose was touched, and gradually she came to make the 'funny' sign in 'funny' situations without any prompting. Although manual babbling did appear to play its part at this stage, it declined as time went on, and its function in the total process of acquiring ASL seems to have been comparatively slight and rather doubtful.

Particularly in the later stages of the learning, imitation was playing a greater and greater part in the process (a fact that in any case could have been anticipated by the striking powers of manual imitation shown by Viki). One of the signs which was clearly corrected by imitation was that for 'flower'. In the acceleration of ASL acquisition, observational learning, as distinct from imitation, was almost certainly the prime factor. But Gardner and Gardner remark (1971), 'However, if Washoe could reach a point at which she asks us for the names of things, then imitative guidance might become the most practical method of introducing new signs.'

Some of the signs developed by Washoe seem to be best described as straight inventions. They are quite different from the signs which had, until then, been modelled for her, and their occurrence throws a particularly strong light upon the animal's mental processes. One example will suffice. The experimenters sometimes could not find an ASL equivalent for an English word which they wished to use. In such cases they would adapt a sign of ASL for the purpose; the sign for 'bib' was one of these cases. They happened to use the ASL sign for 'napkin' or 'wiper' to refer to bibs as well. This sign is made by touching the mouth region with an open hand and a wiping movement. During the eighteenth experimental month, Washoe had begun to use this sign appropriately for bibs, but was still unreliable in its use.

One evening at dinner time, a human companion was holding up a bib and asking Washoe to name it. She tried 'Come-gimme' and 'please', but did not seem to be able to remember the 'bib' sign that we had taught her. Then, she did something very interesting: with the index fingers of both hands she drew an outline of a bib on her chest—starting from behind her neck where the bib should be tied, moving the index fingers down along the outer edge of her chest, and bringing them together again just above her navel.

The authors remark, 'A high level of cognitive ability must be possessed by a creature that can represent the concept of a bib by drawing an outline on its chest with its fingers.'

A number of instances have recently come to light which demonstrate that many animals, at least including the birds and the mammals, must possess greater powers of conceptualization than hitherto seemed credible. Among the pioneers in this field were Herrnstein and Loveland (1964), whose work showed quite dramatically that the domestic pigeon is capable of forming a broad and complex concept when placed in a situation that demands one. The pigeons used by these workers were taught to respond to the presence or absence of human beings in photographs. They were trained to peck one disc if there was any sign of a human being in the photograph, and another if there was no sign. It was found that the most fragmentary, and presumably unfamiliar, aspects of the human being, or parts of the human being, were sufficient to cause the birds to give a positive response. (For similar work on monkeys, see Lehr, 1967.) Accordingly, it was not surprising that the ape Washoe often showed this kind of ability. Many of the items for which Washoe learned the names and the appropriate ASL signals could of course be classified into meaningful groups. Thus, there were six items, 'brush', 'clean soap', 'comb', 'oil', 'lotion', and 'toothbrush', that could be classified as grooming articles; five, namely 'bird', 'bugs', 'cat', 'cow', and 'dog', which could be classified as animals; four 'banana', 'drink', 'meat', and 'sweet', that could be classified as foods, and so on. When Washoe made errors it was possible to show that these were governed by the category of item that was actually presented. Thus in one set of experiments in which Washoe made errors in twelve trials, seven of the twelve were the signs for other items in the appropriate category —in this case the category of grooming articles. Similar results were found for other categories of items. In fact these errors revealed just the kind of conceptualization referred to above.

This was further displayed in Washoe's ability to learn the use of pronouns. When she was being taught, the experimenters often had to use a few specific instances of the appropriate referent: a few items of clothing for 'pants', a few examples of her companions' possessions for 'yours'. When Washoe transferred the sign to another referent, or when she used it in a new combination, she produced examples of the usage that went beyond the ones that had been taught to her. It was from these that it is possible to infer and evaluate her meaning. It would never have been possible to show Washoe all the persons she should designate as 'you', nor all the actions that 'you' was capable of performing. Yet it appeared that Washoe used the pronouns appropriately, that is, for any companion and in combination with a wide variety of signs for action and for attributes. She began to use the two pronouns 'you' and 'me' in January 1968. In spring 1968 she had signed, 'You me out' in a doorway situation and later produced many variants such as

'You Roger Washoe out,' 'You me go out,' 'You me go out hurry.'

At the time of the latest report Washoe has no signs for words that can be used to join members of combinations, such as 'and', 'for', 'with', and 'to'. But perhaps it is significant that words of this type are noticeably absent from the early sentences of young children (Brown and Bellugi, 1964; Brown, 1970).

Washoe, in approximately three years after the experiment commenced, reliably mastered the use of 87 signs included in, or of a type similar to, those which make up ASL. Let us remind ourselves that in a comparable period, the chimpanzee Viki, belonging to Dr. and Mrs. Hayes, acquired a vocabulary of four vocalizations, one of which was still rather doubtful. Nothing further needs to be said to stress the impact and significance of this new approach to the understanding of the communicative abilities of the higher animals.

Syntax in animal communication
We now come to what is in many respects the key question in this whole topic, namely the question of syntax. From what was said above, it will be already clear that the popular notion, derivable from any dictionary, that syntax is a set of rules governing sentence construction will not carry us very far at the present day. In fact Chomsky's *Syntactic Structures* (1957) was, so to speak, a signpost marking the direction of the new road. The problems raised by the advances and developments resulting from the work of Professor Chomsky have been discussed elsewhere (Hinde, 1972) and need not be entered into here.

It is still necessary to enquire, as far as we can, however, whether and in what senses of the word the achievements of Washoe can be described as syntactic. Certainly Washoe combines words meaningfully. In the thirty-eight months following April 1967, the experimenters recorded 294 different two-sign combinations used by this animal. In arriving at this total, different sequences of the same signs, e.g. 'open please' and 'please open', and also 'gimme food' and 'gimme food gimme', were tabulated as the same two-sign combinations. It was soon noticed that the vocabulary seemed to be divided into a small group of words called 'pivots', which are found in the bulk of the two-word utterances, and a larger group which are seldom found in two-word utterances unless they are paired with one of the pivots. All the 87 word signs were scored according to the number of different two-sign combinations in which they appeared. It was found that at least one of the twelve highest-ranking signs occurred in 240 of the 294 different two-sign combinations. These twelve word signs, in descending order of their scores, were 'come', 'gimme', 'please', 'you', 'go', 'me', 'hurry', 'more', 'up', 'open', 'out', 'in', and 'food'.

As the Gardners point out, if the tabulation had been based on the total number of two-sign combinations that Washoe produced, it would indicate only that she had some favourite signs and perhaps some favourite combinations. But in this tabulation each two-sign combination was counted only once, no matter how many times it was used by Washoe, and moreover, reversals of order and repetitions of the same sign were not counted. This indicates that the sample is a sample of types, and the finding that at least one out of a small number of signs appeared in most of the combinations indicates that certain types of combinations were more permissible (according to Washoe's own 'rules') than others. This fact suggests the beginnings of an approach to 'syntax'.

Since Washoe's achievements, significant though they are, are so far removed from the achievements of a fully articulate human being, the Gardners very wisely proceeded by comparing Washoe's two-sign combinations with children's two-word combinations in a way that follows the scheme proposed by Brown (1970). First they listed the 87 signs and grouped them into six categories—one more than in Brown's list. This analysis is shown in Table 5 (p. 66). It will be seen that the six categories, which are 'Appeal', 'Location', 'Action', 'Object', 'Agent', and 'Attribute', overlap to a considerable extent. The addition to the list is the first category, 'Appeal', which seemed necessary to cover Washoe's communications. As Brown suggests, further analysis may make it possible to fit these four 'Appeal' signs, 'gimme', 'hurry', 'more', and 'please', into the other five categories.

A further point of interest appears. Apart from the pronouns 'me' and 'you', most of the readily combined signs are to be found amongst the 'Appeals', 'Locations', and 'Actions'. This suggests that these more readily combined signs serve certain constructive functions. It is quite evident, from a study of the

Table 5
Washoe's signs grouped into six overlapping categories
(From Gardner and Gardner, 1971.)

Appeal	Location	Action			Object				Agent	Attribute
gimme	there	come	bed	look	baby	cheese	hurt	spoon	me	black
hurry	in	go	brush	oil	banana	climb	key	string	you	green
more	out	help	catch	toothbrush	berry	clothes	leaf	sweet	Washoe	red
please	up	hug	clean	ride	bib	cow	light	tree	Dr. G.	white
	down	kiss	comb		bird	dog	meat	window	Mrs. G.	enough
		open	cover		book	flower	pants		Greg	funny
		peek-aboo	dirty		bug	fruit	pencil		Naomi	good
		spin	drink		car	grass	shoes		Roger	quiet
		tickle	food		cat	hammer	smell		Susan	sorry
		listen			chair	hat	smoke		Wende	mine

records of characteristic dialogues between Washoe and one or other of her human associates, that if, in response to an initial word from Washoe (for instance, the sign 'please' or the sign 'come'), the human partner asks the question, 'What you want?' Washoe elaborates by adding a second word in the form of an answer; and this answer expresses considerably more than the initial one-sign utterance. Thus, in response to these questions, the commonly formed two-sign combinations that Washoe uses are as follows: 'please out', 'come open', 'more tickle'. Leading questions indicate what the human partners in this project, Washoe's linguistic community, would accept as completed ASL utterances, and it is clear that she gives them.

Just because infant human beings and infant chimpanzees cannot act as 'informants' in the way that native speakers serve as informants when an unknown human language is being studied, lists of the attempts so far made to analyse children's early language for structure have used the utterances themselves as raw data. And this must obviously be the method employed in the study of the communications between Washoe and her associates. Table 6 (p. 68) compares Washoe's achievements with the structure of the earliest two-word combinations of children. The essence of the scheme for children is the notion that the conjunction of two words can express a relationship that is independent of the particular words in the pair. The comparison set forth in the table is discussed in detail by Gardner and Gardner (1971).

It seems safe, however, to say that Brown's scheme shows that the types of construction which can be distinguished in the earliest combinations of young children express relationships that are somewhat independent of the specific words that appear in the combinations. That is to say, to some extent children's utterances are characterized by structure at this level of development. From the data available to the Gardners, it is estimated that between 70% and 85% of the two-word combinations in the children's samples can be accounted for by the Brown scheme. In the sample of Washoe's 294 two-sign combinations, 228 (or 78%) can be accounted for by the scheme that the Gardners have derived from Brown's. 'At this level of analysis, then, Washoe's earliest two-sign combinations were comparable to the earliest two-word combinations of children.' (Gardner and Gardner, 1971.) There remains the question whether this structure represents the first emergence of syntax or whether it is a

Table 6

Parallel descriptive schemes for the earliest combinations of children and of Washoe
(From Gardner and Gardner, 1971.)

	Brown's (1970) scheme for children			The scheme for Washoe	
Types		**Examples**		**Types**	**Examples**
Attributive:					
Ad+N		big train, red book		Object—Attributable	drink red, comb black
Possessive:				Agent—Attribute	Washoe sorry, Naomi good
N+N		Adam checker, mommy lunch		Agent—Object	clothes Mrs. G., you hat
				Object—Attribute	baby mine, clothes yours
N+V		walk street, go store		Action—Location	go in, look out
				Action—Object	go flower, pants tickle
Locative:				Object—Location	baby down, in hat
N+N		sweater chair, book table			
Agent—Action:					
N+V		Adam put, Eve read		Agent—Action	Roger tickle, you drink
Action—Object:					
V+N		put book, hit ball		Action—Object	tickle Washoe, open blanket
Agent—Object:				Appeal—Action	please tickle, hug hurry
N+N		mommy sock, mommy lunch		Appeal—Object	gimme flower, more fruit

stage of semantic structure that precedes the first stage of truly syntactical construction. The Gardners regard this question as still open.

We may now turn to another recent series of experiments with a chimpanzee using a quite different technique. It will be obvious that the ability to develop an association between two objects or events in contiguity is part of the basic learning repertoire of every animal that can at least establish a conditioned response. Every dog can learn to associate a sound or a gesture with an object which it desires or fears. Premack (1970a,b), in a remarkable series of experiments with 'Sarah', another young female chimpanzee, has developed an ingenious technique for teaching language by means of plastic 'words'. Each 'word' is a metal-backed piece of plastic, of a given and unique combination of shape, size, texture, and colour, which adheres lightly to a magnetized board. Association between the plastic 'word' and the object (e.g. an apple) which it is to represent is readily taught to the animal by simple reward. By an elegant series of steps from this simple beginning, Premack has been able to teach Sarah to 'speak', by tokens, to an extent not inferior to Washoe and in some respects superior. Not only does Sarah's vocabulary now exceed that of Washoe; her use of it is in many respects more sophisticated and complex. Thus Sarah has a vocabulary of 112 plastic 'words' which comprise 8 names of persons (or chimps), 21 verbs, 6 colours, 21 foods, 26 miscellaneous objects, and 30 'concepts, adjectives, and adverbs'.

Exact comparison with Washoe would, of course, be misleading in that the 'words' are made for Sarah; she does not have to learn to make them herself. Nor does she have the free choice of actions open to Washoe; she can manipulate what is given to her but not invent or choose others. Nevertheless, the work with Sarah gives even stronger suggestions of syntax than does that with Washoe. Premack says, 'We feel justified in concluding that Sarah can understand some symmetrical and hierarchical sentence structures and is therefore competent to some degree in the sentence function of language.'

Another achievement of Sarah's that is worthy of mention is her ability to answer questions about her classification of objects. It is possible for instance to ask her, 'A is what to A?' or 'A is what to B?' Two object words are put on the board with the question symbol between them; Sarah's task is to replace the question symbol with the right word, 'same' or 'different'. A second question may be translated, 'A is the same as what?' or 'A is not the same as what?'

Sarah can also be asked a variety of yes–no questions thus: 'Is A the same as A?', 'Is A not the same as A?', and so on. Sarah, it is claimed, learned to answer all three types of questions for an essentially unlimited variety of items, words, and concepts.

There are indeed objections which can be made as to how far these are true questions. This cannot be discussed here, but there is interesting evidence that in such sessions the chimp thinks of the 'word' (say, a piece of blue plastic) not as its literal form but as the thing it represents (e.g. a red apple); just as we, when we hear a familiar word, think immediately of the object it denotes and only exceptionally of the word itself.

Finally we come to the thorny question of language and its relation to speech. The general colloquial use of the term 'language' is so vague as to be of little value. But there has been for many years a widespread tendency, among both students of animal behaviour and a good many physiological psychologists (such as Teuber, 1967), to use the term language for many of the more elaborate examples of communication amongst animals, especially for the transfer of social information and particularly when the transfer is vocal or auditory. While there is much to be said for this, the usage in the past has perhaps been too naïve (Thorpe, 1968). Hebb and Thompson (1954) propose that the minimal criterion of language is twofold. First, language combines two or more representative gestures or noises purposefully for a single effect. Secondly, it uses the same gestures in different combination for different effects, changing readily with circumstances. It will by now have become quite obvious that not only the communication of Washoe with her associates but also the communication of many birds and some other animals come within this definition of language. There remains, however, the problem of intent or purpose. To express my own view, I would say that no one who has worked for a long period with a higher animal, such as a chimpanzee, particularly in the circumstances of the Gardners' work, is justified in doubting the purposiveness of such communication. I believe such purposiveness is also clear to the experienced and open-minded observer with many of the Canidae, with some (probably many) other mammals, and with certain birds (Thorpe, 1966, 1969).

Chomsky's view of language as evidence for 'mentality'

One of the reasons why it has been ncessary to consider so carefully the question of animal languages is because it relates to the arguments put forward by Chomsky (1967, 1971) and others (Lyons in Hinde, 1972) that the possession of language is indubitable evidence of mentality and some basic and 'innate' mental structure (deep structures) without which the acquisition of true language, whether by animals or men, is inconceivable.[1] Consequently, the work we have been discussing, particularly that with chimpanzees, gives very strong *a priori* reasons for the assumption that 'mind' has indeed developed, during the course of evolution in, at the very least, the higher mammals. This conclusion will lead us on to the chapter which follows. And this, in itself, raises the perennial problem of drawing hard and fast lines of demarcation in considering the realms of the mind. One of the tasks of the scientific student of animal behaviour is to attempt to establish whether or not there are such lines, and if so, what and where they are.

The pioneer work with Washoe and Sarah has led recently to an increasing flow of results of a similar nature from a number of different laboratories (see Rumbaugh, Gill, and von Glasserfeld, 1973; Rumbaugh *et al.*, 1973; Fouts, 1972). Rumbaugh's chimp 'Lana' works at a specially designed 'typewriter' having a keyboard of 50 keys, each marked with a different coloured symbol and linked with a computer. The computer flashes the symbols she has typed on to a screen in front of her, at the same time analysing the sequences she types and making a permanent record of all interactions. Through this device Lana asks for, and gets, all her food and drink, a look outside, music, toys, films, and human companionship. One particular transaction with her teacher 'Tim' is significant. Tim has just entered with a container, of a type unknown to Lana, holding sweets.

Lana: Tim give Lana name of this?
Tim: Box name of this.
Lana: Yes. Tim give this box?
Tim: Yes. (*Lana takes box and takes out sweets.*)

1. For further elucidation of the thorny question of the nature of language and for Chomsky's changing views on animal communication, see Hinde, 1972, Chapters 1–6, and especially references to Lyons, Chomsky, and Thorpe.

As a result of the totality of chimpanzee experiments nearly all the critical objections raised by scientists against crediting animals with true linguistic developments have now been answered by at least one animal; and most of them by several. These objections amounted to a demand for the fulfilment of the following criteria, namely that an animal must:

1. Demonstrate an extensive system of names for objects in the environment.

2. Sign about objects which are not physically present.

3. Use signs for concepts—not just for objects, actions, and agents.

4. Invent semantically appropriate combinations.

5. Use correct order when it is semantically necessary.

(For a valuable recent summary of this work, see Fleming, 1975.)

This shows that we are even now only at the beginning of the application of an important and powerful new technique from which we stand to learn much in years to come. I believe that no one should have anything to fear from its cautious and objective application. Personally, I think it is safe to conclude that, if chimpanzees had the necessary equipment in the larynx and pharynx, they could learn to talk at least as well as can children of three years of age, and perhaps older.

The next question is, 'Could they count?' The answer is, I believe, 'Yes, up to the number seven.' This problem will be next considered.

We must recognize a fact that is too often forgotten, namely that visual signals are as important and as complex in man as in any animal. And many domestic animals, even though they may have little power in understanding the niceties of vocal communication, can nevertheless often recognize the intentions of their masters by observation of minute involuntary gestures or expressions, with uncanny precision—as was shown by the famous 'calculating horses' that so puzzled comparative psychologists in the early years of this century. What, then, is the difference, if any, between such visual signals and the language of human beings? It is not merely a question of symbolism because, as every ethologist knows, the visual signals of animals may become so reduced as to be little more than 'symbolic'. I have seen a bull European bison (*Bison bonasus*) intimidate a junior and subordinate male in its herd by the very slightest sideways flick of its head, indicative of the tossing and goring movements. Nor is it, as used to be argued, that animal language is emotive only, whilst human language is supposed to be emotive and propositional.

The problem of abstraction

We may ask then, does the human ability to symbolize—in the sense of representing completely abstract or general ideas by words which in themselves have nothing of the essential characteristics of the concepts which they denote—provide us with a difference? For example, the word 'two' has nothing double about it, nor is the word 'five' quintuple; but man can learn to understand absolutely general meanings of this kind. Can animals do the same? As far as we know for certain, no animal language, however much information it may convey, involves the learnt realization of completely general abstractions. Otto Koehler and his pupils, in their famous studies of the recognition of numbers, showed that animals, especially birds, can 'think unnamed numbers'—that is (and this is also true of squirrels and some other mammals), they have a prelinguistic number sense; to some extent they think without words. Some examples of their number-training, however, do appear to involve something more than a special association between given numbers and particular signals, and there is now some evidence for the ability of birds to arrive at a general solution indicating the comprehension of a numerical series.

Lögler (1943) carried the investigation of the problem of number sense in animals a step further by extremely painstaking work on counting in a grey parrot. Extending the earlier investigation of Koehler and his pupils, he found that this parrot, 'Jako', was able to recognize the successive presentation of a number of optic stimuli as a signal for the task of performing the same number of actions. The bird, having been shown, say, four or six or seven light-flashes, was then able to take four or six or seven (as the case might be) of irregularly distributed baits out of a row of food trays. Not even numerous random changes in the temporal sequence of signal stimuli impaired the percentage of correct solutions. Having learnt this task, a signal of successive light-flashes was replaced by successive notes of a flute. The bird was, however, able to substitute immediately, without further training, and the change from light-flashes to flute notes had no effect on the number of correct solutions. Nor was the accomplishment hindered by the completely arhythmic presentation of stimuli, or by a change of pitch. This parrot was not able to accomplish a task which represented a combination of the two faculties of learning numbers presented successively and simultaneously. For example, he could not respond to numbers presented visually and simultaneously after hearing the same number of acoustic stimuli presented successively—yet when he had learnt to 'act upon' two or one, after hearing two sounds simultaneously or a single sound, he was spontaneously able to open a lid with two spots on it or a lid with one spot, according to the same acoustic signals. That is to say, he was able to transpose from the simultaneous-successive combination to the simultaneous-simultaneous in twenty experiments without relearning. It seems, then, that this remarkable work brings our estimate of the counting achievements of birds a step nearer that of man, though of course it is still not true counting in the fully human sense.

Also of great interest is the extensive work of Rensch (1962, 1967), in which he found that a civet cat (*Viverricula malaccensis*) could learn to choose between pairs of patterns, one composed of even, the other of odd, numbers of spots or signs of various sorts, but otherwise having nothing in common, thus suggesting averbal concepts of odd and even.

Behaviour, a jump ahead of structure
Perhaps the most reasonable assumption at present is that, however great the gulf which divides animal communication systems from human language, there is no single characteristic which can be used as an infallible criterion for distinguishing between animals and men in this respect. Human speech is unique only in the way in which it combines and extends attributes which, in themselves, are not peculiar to man, but are found also in more than one group of animals. We have evidence that animals can use conceptual symbols, but to a limited degree; and that here, as in so many other instances, the difference between the minds of animals and men seems to be one of degree—often the degree of abstraction that can be achieved—rather than one of kind. But man can manipulate abstract symbols to an extent far in excess of any animal, and that is the difference between bird 'counting' and our mathematics. I think we can sum up this matter by saying that although no animal appears to have a

language which is propositional, fully syntactic, and at the same time clearly expressive of intention, all these features can be found separately (to at least some degree) in the animal kingdom. Consequently, bearing in mind the work on chimps discussed above, we can say that the distinction between man and animals, on the ground that only the former possess 'true language', seems far less defensible than heretofore. Yet, there comes a point where 'more' creates a 'difference'.

If we try to look back dispassionately at the animal performances described in this chapter (and they constitute but a tithe of the striking facts which could have been relevantly discussed), we find ourselves increasingly convinced that, astounding though the mechanisms studied and revealed by anatomists and physiologists are, something more than what we can call 'mechanism' is required to account for some at least of these overwhelming performances of animals and their evolutionary development. In the latter stages of this evolutionary progress, to say the least, it seems to me that we must agree with the conclusion alluded to earlier: that behaviour is always a jump ahead of structure; and that habits, traditions, and behavioural inventions must have played an ever increasing role in the evolutionary story as the animals mounted the ladder of complexity.[1] Such formative forces helped them to achieve ever new adjustments, mental and physical, adapted them more and more, each to its peculiar niche, and enabled them increasingly to control the environment thereof—a course which has led to man's present, and in some ways disastrous, domination of the globe.

1. R. Dawkins, in his sprightly and stimulating book, *The selfish gene* (Oxford University Press, Oxford, 1976), disclaims all knowledge of philosophy but is, of course, aware that his title is simply a clever gimmick—for only an extreme 'mentalist' could assume that a gene has the experience of being selfish. But he does seem to maintain that all evolution is solely based on gene survival *until* man is reached. With the coming of man, however, and the concomitant evolution of subjective consciousness—which he regards as the most profound mystery facing modern biology—we find 'memes', which in some respects take over from genes. Memes include ideas, concepts, beliefs, arts, and technologies, which spread through our society as cultural traditions; and which, even in comparatively illiterate tribes, are passed on from generation to generation. This restriction of memes to man amounts to saying that, from the evolutionary point of view, we can afford to ignore all the evidence for consciousness in animals; and the consequent development of primitive proto-cultures, as in primates.

References to Chapter 3

This chapter is largely a summary and abbreviation of relevant sections of:

Thorpe, W. H. (1974) *Animal nature and human nature*, Methuen, London, and Doubleday-Anchor, New York.

Detailed references to almost all the authorities cited in the chapter will be found in the above and/or in:

Hinde, R. A. (ed.) (1972) *Non-verbal communication*, Cambridge University Press, Cambridge and London. (See especially Chs. 1, 2, 5, and 6.)

References which are mostly too recent to be found in the above works are as follows:

Fleming, E. (1975) 'The state of the ape', *Psychology today* **1**, 16–25.

Fouts, R. C. (1972) 'Use of guidance in teaching sign-language to a chimpanzee', *J. Comp. & Physiol. Psychol.* **80**, 515–22.

Rumbaugh, D. M., Gill, T. V., and von Glasserfeld, E. C. (1973) 'Reading and sentence completion by a chimpanzee (*Pan satyrus*)', *Science* **182**, 731–3.

Rumbaugh, D. M., *et al.* (1973) 'A computer-controlled language-training system for investigating the language skills of young apes', *Behav. Rsch. Methods and Instrumentation* **5**, 385–92.

4
Problems of consciousness

The uniqueness of man

From what has gone before my readers may well have begun to wonder how far, if at all, man can still be regarded as unique. It used to be said—and not so very long ago either—that animals can neither learn, plan ahead, nor conceptualize. In addition to this it was argued that animals cannot use, much less make, tools, that they have no language, and that they cannot count. It was argued that they also lack all artistic sense and all ethical sense.

The first six of these eight supposed differences are now almost completely discredited, as will have been perfectly clear from the preceding chapters. It is true that I have not dealt particularly with the question of using and making tools, but there are now a considerable number of well attested instances of animals using tools and, in captivity, making tools. Moreover, in the wild, chimpanzees are known to prepare very simple stick tools for use in the collection of termites ('white ants') as food, by choosing particular kinds of trees, breaking off twigs of the right length, removing side branches, leaves, etc., before proceeding on their hunting expeditions.

Reflective consciousness and abstract problem-solving in man

Yet I am still of the absolute conviction that man is unique in his nature and achievements. The evidence centres round two considerations: first, the degree of the development of man's language from the most complete and convincing language we know of in animals, and secondly, his possession of fully reflective self-consciousness. This amounts to saying that man is, to use Sir John Eccles's term, an 'experiencing self' in a way and to a degree which transcends entirely the self-experiencing of animals and does indeed give man a unique position. Now of course, we are always up against the difficulty, as in so many other problems, of knowing exactly when and where a difference in degree spills over into a difference in kind. In Whitehead's last book, *Modes of Thought* (1938), he says, 'The distinction between man and animals is in one sense only a difference of degree. But the extent of the degree makes all the difference. The Rubicon has been crossed.' As will become apparent, I find it necessary to assume, in looking at the evolution story and the questions of the origin of man, the origin of life, and the establishment of self-reflective consciousness, that we do repeatedly come up against evidence for the emergence of truly new values. In other words 'more' is sometimes 'different'. And I believe this is what Whitehead implies by the quotation I have given—that there comes a point at which a difference of degree brings into operation new laws and requires new concepts which were previously inconceivable, however great our knowledge; and that this 'emergence' is what Whitehead has in mind when he says, 'The Rubicon has been crossed.' And so I believe that the possession of a fully self-reflecting personality, an experiencing self, is the outstanding characteristic on which depends the uniqueness of man and from which all else follows.

Popper points out that 'problem-solving' is an idea which is totally meaningless in the inanimate world, and which seems to have appeared together with life and increased in range and complexity as we go up the animal scale. Here again we have the emergence of a new quality with man—for the reflective and abstract problem-solving involved in, for instance, the higher ranges of mathematics and in logical philosophy is surely something which has no real counterpart in the animal world.

Thus I believe that from the uniqueness of man's experiencing self arise all the other characteristics in which he can be considered as unique: imagination, art in all its forms, the sense of values held to be absolute, the free will to choose between values, the moral sense in all its ramifications, philosophy (including scientific theories), religion, the concepts of the soul and of deity, and the knowledge of death.

Even to make a beginning at a detailed appraisal of man's uniqueness would require another chapter, if not another book. But one must specify one supremely important central facet of man's uniqueness, and that is his sense of the infinite. Koestler has developed this in more than one of his works (but notably in

The Ghost in the Machine, 1967), pointing out that the history of science shows that the great innovators have always been aware of the transparence of the phenomena of the physical world towards a different and basic order of reality. This is why science, if it is to be true to itself, always needs a metaphysic to maintain and secure this relation to the infinite—for without it, a scientist, however good a technician he may be, cannot be a true savant. As one of the greatest biologists, Louis Pasteur, said, 'I see everywhere in the world the inevitable expression of the concept of infinity. . . . The idea of God is nothing more than one form of the idea of infinity. . . . The ideals of art, of science, are lighted by reflection from the infinite.' (Quoted by Dubos, 1951.)

The question of death-awareness is of especial interest to the ethologist in that no one has yet produced any convincing reason for believing animals to be aware of their mortality. Although there are odd observations here and there of behaviour which suggest it, so far these lack both credibility and effective confirmation. So we cannot discuss this further here—but, to put it imaginatively, the animals are still in Paradise with no experience of the Fall.[1]

After this brief introductory survey let us look again at language. As we have seen from the last chapter, a great deal of animal behaviour, including the various forms of animal language, has an expressive function (giving expression to the internal states of an animal) and a communicative (or signalling) function. But Sir Karl Popper has argued, I think rightly, that human language has a basic descriptive function which is absent from animal language—except in so far as the dance of the honey-bees is descriptive of a particular situation—and that human language has also an argumentative function. I suppose

1. Save, perhaps, such unfortunate domestic animals as, having possibly attained a glimpse into the mind of a loved but unworthy master (one of their 'own Gods', to use Rudyard Kipling's phrase), find his 'love' to be fickle, careless, and cruel rather than steadfast, patient, and true, as they had come to believe. This is to suggest that a cherished domestic animal may perhaps have entered upon the first steps of 'soul-making'; and Kipling again, with true poetic insight, makes his dog speak of 'this dim half-soul which hurts me so!' (*Thy Servant a Dog*, 1930.) This may be nonsense; but nevertheless it may serve as a warning to people of the seriousness of undertaking 'own-God status' to an affectionate and trusting pet such as a dog, whose capacity as a member of a highly social species they may, through ignorance, completely underestimate.

one could describe animal conflicts over territorial boundaries as 'argumentative', but to do so would, I think, be using that word in a misleading and unwarranted sense. A reasoned argument is surely something over and above a simple quarrel over possession. 'Argument' implies ethical or moral reasons for 'rightness' or 'wrongness'; whereas animals' territory disputes amount to little more than assertions that possession is nine points of the law.

This question of what one might call the transcendental qualities of human language leads to another crucial matter—namely how far we consider that the mental, moral, and philosophical attributes of man's thought and speech necessitate some form of dualistic attitude to the world. This will be more profitably discussed after we have considered the psychological and physiological evidence for the experiencing self as being at the basis of our view of the world.

Levels of conscious experience
We now come to consider the activity of the brain and its relation to conscious experience. This question of the nature of what one might call the structure of the world of consciousness has been the subject of prolonged and profound discussion by both philosophers and physiologists. In what I have to say on the subject I have been particularly influenced by Lashley and Eccles as physiologists and by Polten and Popper as philosophers.

Polten considers conscious experience at three levels. Eccles has conveniently summarized this in the accompanying diagram (Fig. 8). First, there is outer sensing, which is the perceptual experience due to input from sense-organs, not only from the external world by extero-receptors such as the organs of sight, hearing, smell, taste, and touch, but also from body states, for example, by proprioceptors from muscles, joints, etc., and by receptors for pain, hunger, thirst, etc.

Secondly, there is inner sensing, which is not directly derived from sense data, though it is often triggered by these data and has many derivatives from them. It includes the experiences of thinking—emotions, dispositional intentions, memories, dreams, and creative imagination.

Thirdly, there is the pure 'ego' or 'self', which recognizes itself by apperception (Kant) and is central to all experience. It transcends immediate experiences and gives each of us the sense of continuity throughout a lifetime. This sense of continuity bridges

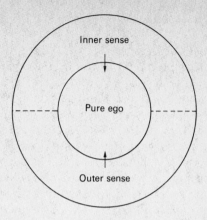

Outer Sense	Inner Sense	Pure Ego
Light	Thoughts	The self
Colour	Feelings	The soul
Sound	Memories	
Smell	Dreams	
Taste	Imaginings	
Pain	Intentions	
Touch		

Fig. 8: World of consciousness. Diagram of the three postulated components in the world of consciousness, together with a tabulated list of their constituents. (From Eccles, 1974.)

periods of unconsciousness as in sleep and as a result of brain injury or anaesthetics. But, as Eccles says, 'It is essential to the concept each of us has of being a self,' and he adds, 'in the religious sense it corresponds to the soul.' The pure ego implies in some rather vague sense the fusion of the totality of the impressions, thoughts, and feelings which weld a person's conscious being into a single whole; that is, a belief in an internal perceiving agent, an 'I' or 'self' which does the perceiving. So we come inevitably to the conclusion that this agent selects and unifies elements into a unique field of consciousness, with the subsequent implications, first, that the self transcends time and space, since memory brings into immediate relations events remote from one another in these dimensions, and secondly, that in man it makes possible the creation of ethical and aesthetic values held to be absolute.

Consciousness and brain-states

Now follows the question, 'How far are these various levels of conscious experience related to brain-states?' The materialist-behaviourist answer was that this question was meaningless; there were only brain-states and the rest was introspective fantasy and as such could be ignored. We have already discussed one aspect of this, namely that it is self-stultifying—for how can brain-states provide a complete up-to-date description of themselves? So, as a philosophy it is discredited. As we shall see, one part of the brain can certainly process the information in another; but this is a very different matter from the provision of a complete representation.

The modern behaviourism of Skinner (1971) is hardly more sensible. Although he does not deny conscious experiences, he relegates them to a meaningless role with respect to the behaviour of both man and animals. This is absurd because it resolves the brain–mind problem by ignoring both brain and mind. Skinner's approach remains, as it has always been, completely anti-physiological: considering the brain as unavailable to useful study, as if it were enclosed in a black box which could in no way be penetrated, and reducing the mind to utter ineffectiveness.

As I have argued elsewhere (Thorpe, 1974), the acceptance of material entities as real but dismissal of mental entities as abstractions is patently absurd. Nevertheless, it still seems to attract quite a number of physiologists, including even some learned and distinguished ones, and still more scientists who have not thought at all deeply about the matter. One can only suppose that they are in some way bemused by the practical economy, tidiness, and convenience of it, even though the whole thing is spurious. We are in fact left with only two alternatives. The first is that there is a two-way interaction between mental and physical events. The second is the double-aspect theory (now usually known as the identity hypothesis), which asserts that certain events are, at one and the same time, both mental and material, the mental being the interior view of what has a physical exterior.

This double-aspect theory has, however, suffered as a result of the remarkable investigations on human subjects by Sperry and his associates. His view is that phenomenal experience is not identical with, but is informationally coherent with, observed neural events. That is to say, as physiologists tend to suppose, that there must always be some physiological events in the brain, at any one time, running parallel with what we experience. This, of course, is not to say that brain-states always give rise to conscious experience—a view which can clearly be shown to be false.

The cerebral cortex

It is essential to start our consideration of the relationship between brain-states and consciousness by giving a brief outline, in words as non-technical as possible, of the neuronal mechanisms involved. Here we should say that the progress of brain neurology during the last twenty-five years or so, has been such as to reveal a complexity beyond imagining. From this it follows that all the early writings on the brain–mind problem, many of which set forth self-assured and very simplistic accounts of brain function, are outmoded.

The essential structure of the brain, from our present point of view, is the cerebral cortex, which is the folded surface sheet of densely packed nerve cells that are estimated to number about ten thousand million. These cells communicate with each other by particular regions of close contact, called synapses. Each cell receives many thousands of these contacts by branches (axons) coming from other nerve cells, and in turn each nerve cell influences many hundreds or thousands of other nerve cells when it is triggered to discharge an impulse along its efferent pathway, the axon, with its numerous branches (Eccles, 1966; 1970, p. 153). At first glance the cerebral cortex appears as a neuronal network somewhat like a vast telephone exchange of ten thousand million elements—each nerve cell having converging on to it contacts with hundreds of other nerve cells and each nerve cell in its turn spreading its influence by divergence over hundreds of other nerve cells. It is now well established that there are two kinds of junctions or synapses. One is excitatory; and if there is sufficiently intense bombardment by excitatory synapses, the recipient nerve cell will be stimulated to discharge impulses along its own axon. The other kind of synapse is inhibitory. These counteract the excitatory connections and tend to silence the nerve cell which receives them. Thus each nerve cell is continually subjected to bombardment by these two types of stimulus, and so its responses derive very largely from the total impact of its neighbours upon it.

It is also well known that the essential time of action of the nerve cell, in an operative linkage, is about one-thousandth of a second for cells with short axons. This represents the total time that elapses between the reception of the excitation that triggers the discharge and the action of this impulse on other nerve cells. Thus, once activity arises in a population of nerve cells, it is potentially capable of almost explosive spread throughout the neuronal network—through millions of cells in a few milliseconds. And as Eccles says, 'Inhibitory synaptic activity mercifully can restrain this explosive spread which would otherwise result in a convulsion.' He adds that it is still impossible to conceive the manner of operation of the neuronal network in a more global manner, involving tens of millions of neurones, which is continually proceeding in the cerebral cortex during all kinds of conscious experiences such as memories, thoughts, dispositional intentions, and so forth. This account concerns the cerebral cortex alone, but it is enough to show what a staggering problem in neurophysiology the attempt to understand the action of the brain involves.

When we look at the way in which the brain is informed of what goes on in the external world (which may, of course, be external or internal to the body), things are not quite so difficult. Electromagnetic radiations with wavelengths between about 400 and 700 microns are transduced in the retina to give discharges of nerve impulses along the optic nerve fibres. These are brief all-or-nothing electrical events which travel along a million or so nerve fibres in the optic pathway without any interference in the way of cross-talk from their neighbours. Information from a sense-organ, such as the retina, is transmitted to the visual cortex in coded form, both by the frequency of impulse-repetition in the fibre and by the topographic relationship of retinal origin and of cortical termination. This afferent pathway, which is in effect the optic nerve, does not connect retinal point to cortical point, but signals more symmetrical geometrical arrangements such as edges, lines, angular orientations, and so forth.

What can we imagine to be proceeding in the machinery of the cerebral cortex when some image is projected on the retina? Essentially there are bursts of discharges in cells responding to

lines or edges in the visual field and in various specific orientations. This itself is quite a complex business when we realize that
there are three hundred million neurons in the visual cortex
alone. There are cells which are particularly sensitive and respon-
sive to lengths and widths, lines and slits, angles, and so on. It
looks as though, in due course, cells will be found responding to
more and more complex patterns; and it may be that eventually
cells will be discovered which selectively respond to abstract
forms, such as triangularity. It this happens, it will to some
extent explain our ability to recognize abstract forms (Eccles,
1970, p. 160).

Let me here quote Sherrington (1940): 'We might imagine this
principle [of integration] pursued to culmination in final
supreme convergence on one ultimate pontifical nerve cell, a cell
the climax of the whole system of integration.' This indeed would
be a reasonable supposition in view of the fact that the phenomenon of hierarchy is very obvious when we study the behaviour
of the nervous system. Sherrington continues,

Such would be a spatial climax to a system of centralisation; it would
secure integration by receiving all and dispensing all, as unitary
arbiter of a totalitarian state. But convergence towards the brain
offers in fact nothing of that kind. The brain region, which we may
call 'mental', is not a concentration into one cell but an enormous
expansion into millions of cells. They are, it is true, richly inter-
connected. But where it is a question of 'mind', the nervous system
does not integrate itself by centralisation upon one pontifical cell.
Rather it elaborates a millionfold democracy whose each unit is a
cell.

As Eccles says, the dynamic properties of patterned activity in
tens of millions of neurons with the connectives that we have
been describing defeat not only the imagination but, so far, any
attempt at mathematical treatment. However, there are stimulating new theories now in the field which may in due course
revolutionize our approach to the subject.

It must be emphasized once again that there is no immediate
experience of a perception when the visual cortex is activated.
This is just one stage on the way to the much more elaborate
patterned activity that must be associated with consciousness.
It is interesting to note that these initial stages of activation,
namely the electrical responses of the cortex, are unaltered even

in relatively deep anaesthesia; and, with just perceptible flashes
of light, at least 0·2 seconds of cortical activity may be needed
before a perception is registered. Professor Libet and his colleagues in the Department of Physiology at the University of
California, San Francisco, have found in their work on that part
of the cerebral cortex which is sensitive to stimulation of the
surface of the body, that there was a delay of at least half a
second before the onset of the experienced sensation whatever
the conditions of threshold stimulation. So, clearly, there is time
for an enormous elaboration of neural activity in the most complex spatio-temporal patterns during what is called the 'incuba-
tion period' of conscious experience at threshold level. This implies what is well known from the detailed work of Moruzzi (see
Eccles, 1966), that only an extremely small fraction of the total
sensory impact on our brains is actually experienced. For example, during sleep there is a continuing overall activity of cortical
cells, and in some regions there may even be increased activity at
that time.

Consciousness and perception of position and movement
Another aspect of the problem of consciousness is approached
by modern physiological studies on the old problem of sensation
and perception. Gibson (1966) quotes with approval Thomas
Reid's (1785) statement that 'the external senses have a double
province; to make us feel and to make us perceive; to furnish us
with a variety of sensations and to give us a conception of external objects'. Yet Gibson himself has argued that sensations are
not the basis of perception but rather that, as William James
postulated, perception is primary whereas sensations are secon-
darily isolated parts thereof, at least in mature human beings,
which is also the traditional view of the Gestalt psychologists.
But it may be that, in the more primitive animals, the beginning
of consciousness was in some way connected with the first
appearance of the ability to combine different sensory modalities
to provide an elementary map of the environment so that, for
the first time in evolutionary history, animals could 'find their
way about'. (See Thorpe, 1963; Pantin, 1968.) In that it suggests
that the development of proprioception (perception of position
and movement) marks an especially important stage, this view
receives much support from recent work in the U.S.S.R., summarized by Razran (1971), who, in modern neurophysiological

jargon, expresses views not much different from those of Thomas Reid quoted above. Razran goes on to propound the conclusion that the liminal consciousness of a sensation is anchored to a particular sensory modality or quality, whereas perception is largely inter-modal or rather super-modal in quality. He also quotes with approval Gibson's statement that 'proprioception or self-sensitivity is . . . an overall function, common to all systems, not a special sense and that the activity of orienting, exploring, and selecting, extracts the external and internal information from the stimulus flux while registering the change as subjective feeling'.

This highly simplified and very brief account of the development of a conscious experience will serve to refute dramatically the view implied by the identity hypothesis (at least in its earlier and rather naïve forms) that as soon as neural activity lights up in the cerebral cortex there is a conscious experience. In fact, there is an intense ongoing activity in the cortex of the awake subject in the total absence of any specific sensory inputs; and as everyone knows there is even activity during sleep, an activity which is enhanced during periods of dreaming. So it is clear that time is required both for synaptic transmission and the enormous development and elaboration of neural patterns which are apparently needed to establish conscious experience.

Conscious intention

It must be recognized that intention comes into the picture. Only a very small fraction of the complex ongoing patterned response of the cerebral neurons is experienced. The remainder fades away unobserved; and of course it is essential that it should do so, for one can imagine the confusion that would result if we actually experienced the totality of the cerebral patterns in our cortex. A very obvious feature of our conscious experience is that with training and learning, from infancy upwards, we have the power of relegating many very elaborate actions and responses to the subconscious or unconscious levels where they are, so to speak, so automated that they can take charge of an enormous preponderance of our life's activities, to our great relief and contentment. Everyone knows how car driving becomes automatic, just as does piano playing (at a relatively artistic level), with the result that we can drive while at the same time conversing and observing the scenery, with just enough unconscious or subconscious attention to the highway to arrive safely. Then, when an accident threatens, suddenly consciousness takes over; and many who have been in this unenviable situation, report that time seems suddenly to have stretched until seconds apparently become minutes so that at least we feel we have ample time to decide on the best strategy.

The neurophysiology of conscious experience
The complexity I have just referred to is peculiarly highlighted by work of only the last five years or so—especially that of Sperry and his associates. This has arisen out of the discovery that many cases of severe and repeated epileptic seizures can be greatly ameliorated, if not cured, by the operation of cutting the great cerebral commissure, the *corpus callosum*, which provides for communication between the two cerebral hemispheres. It has long been known that one of these hemispheres is dominant and is the 'speech' hemisphere (almost always the left one); and Sperry's cases have shown that only the input from receptor organs to the dominant hemisphere gives conscious experiences to the operated subject. For example, the patient knows nothing of signs which are flashed on to the left visual field or of touch and movement of the left hand; for these are exclusively projected to the right (minor) hemisphere. The subject's ignorance of all the perceptual inputs to the minor hemisphere is complete. He is able to carry out with the left hand appropriate and skilled actions deriving from such inputs. But if the surgeon points out to the subject that his left hand has carried out appropriate and intelligent actions all he can reply is, 'It must have been a guess or an unconscious accident;' he never says that it is the result of his own experience and understanding. Such a patient, with the *corpus callosum* severed, has no voluntary control over the left hand. If questioned he makes such statements as 'I cannot work with that hand' or that 'the hand is numb'. The whole perceptual side of the minor hemisphere remains impenetrable when an attempt is made to discover whether there are some mental attributes associated with all the skill and correct responses programmed from the minor hemisphere.

Fig. 9 shows the extraordinary division between the two hemispheres' abilities and functions. Since this diagram was prepared it has been found that the minor hemisphere can only recognize

Dominant hemisphere	Minor hemisphere
Liaison to consciousness	No such liaison
Verbal	Almost non-verbal Musical
Ideational	Pictorial and pattern sense
Analytic	Synthetic
Sequential	Holistic
Arithmetical and computer-like	Geometrical and spatial

Fig. 9: The principal specific performances of the dominant and minor hemispheres as suggested by the new conceptual developments of Levy-Agresti and Sperry (1968). (From Eccles, 1974.)

nouns (which was implied by labelling it as 'almost non-verbal') whereas the Wernicke Area on the left side, namely the dominant hemisphere, gives meaning to sentences (see Fig. 10, p. 91). It is suggested that the division of tasks shown in this diagram enables each hemisphere to perform its particular general mode of processing information before there is synthesis and eventual appearance as a conscious experience. Since neural events in the minor hemisphere do not directly give the subject conscious experiences, it is necessary to postulate that the neuronal machinery concerned in these specific operational tasks works at an unconscious level; which would be in good accord with the psychiatric concept of the unconscious mind. For example, as argued by Levy-Agresti and Sperry (1968), in listening to music we can suppose that immense and complex operational tasks, such as decoding, synthesizing, and patterning, are carried out in the temporal lobe of the minor hemisphere. It is then suggested that the communication via the *corpus callosum* to the liaison areas of the dominant hemisphere, only from which can the conscious experiences arise, is presumably delayed until these most sophisticated neural operations have been carried out in the special musical centres.

Eccles stresses (1974) that the transmission in the *corpus callosum* is not a simple one-way affair. There are no less than 200 million fibres in this tract, and they must carry a fantastic wealth of impulse traffic in both directions. In the normal operation of the cerebral hemispheres, activity of any one part of the hemisphere is as effectively and rapidly transmitted to the other hemisphere as to another lobe of the same hemisphere. The whole cerebrum thus achieves a most effective unity; and thus transection of the *corpus callosum* gives a unique and complete cleavage of this unity—for the neural activities of the minor hemisphere are isolated from those cerebral areas which give and receive from the conscious self. After the operation the conscious self is recognizably the same self or person as existed before the brain-splitting operation and retains the unity of self-consciousness and mental singleness unimpaired. However, in the operated patient this unity is at the expense of unconsciousness of all happenings in the minor, right hemisphere (see Fig. 13, p. 98).

The human brain's mechanism for consciousness
So there is strong evidence that we must associate with the dominant hemisphere, which as we have seen is the speech hemisphere, the amazing property of being able to give rise to conscious experiences in perception and also to receive from them in the carrying out of willed movements. This remarkable association of speech and consciousness with the dominant hemisphere naturally gave rise to the question as to whether there was some special anatomical structure in this hemisphere which was lacking in the other. Until recently, and even now in general, the two hemispheres are regarded as being, anatomically, mirror images at least at a crude level. But recently it has been discovered (see Figs. 10 and 11) that in about 80 per cent of human brains there are asymmetries with special developments of the cerebral cortex in the regions of both the posterior and the anterior speech areas. So one may assume specially refined structural and functional properties as the basis for the linguistic performance of these areas; but this has yet to be investigated with modern electron-microscopic techniques.

It was discovered in 1973 (Wada *et al.*) that the seven-month foetus has already developed hypertrophy of the eventual speech areas. This is to say that genetic instructions are building the

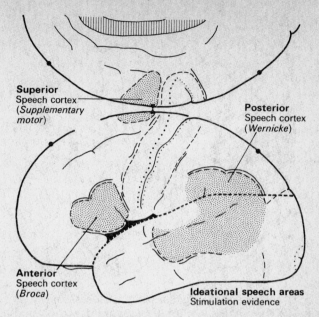

Superior
Speech cortex
(*Supplementary
motor*)

Posterior
Speech cortex
(*Wernicke*)

Anterior
Speech cortex
(*Broca*)

Ideational speech areas
Stimulation evidence

Fig. 10: Cortical speech areas of the dominant hemisphere in the
human brain as determined by electrical interference. (From Eccles,
1974, after Penfield, 1966.)

speech areas long before they are to be used; which implies that
'The human brain at the stage of the infant is already giving
evidence of incipient speech performance.' But the pattern of
organization is not fixed at this stage, for damage to the potential
speech hemisphere at an early stage can result in the other, un-
damaged hemisphere becoming the speech hemisphere. This
transfer, however, may not always happen. 'A hemisphere
severely damaged in infancy may still develop as a speech
hemisphere.'[1]

1. In this connection it is of great interest that studies now under way at
   the Department of Psychology of the University of Edinburgh by Tre-
   varthen and Murray have revealed complex patterns of communication
   behaviour in infants less than two months of age. These include 'pre-
   speech' (rudiments of speaking) and sign-making with the hands. By
   this means rudimentary conversations between baby and mother can
   take place and these have complex emotional effects on both parties. It
   is also claimed to be certain that at two months the activities which the
   baby directs towards people are more elaborate than any he may direct
   towards the physical or impersonal world.

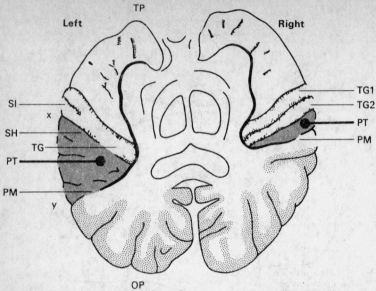

Fig. 11: Upper surfaces of human temporal lobes exposed by a cut on each side. Typical left–right differences are shown. The posterior margin (PM) of the planum temporale (PT) slopes backward more sharply on the left than on the right, so that the end 'y' of the left Sylvian fissure lies posterior to the corresponding point on the right. The anterior margin of the sulcus of Heschl (SH) slopes forward more sharply on the left. In this brain there is a single traverse gyrus of Heschl (TG) on the left and two on the right (TG1, TG2). TP, temporal pole; OP, occipital pole; SI, sulcus intermedius of Beck. (From Eccles, 1974, after Geschwind and Levitsky, 1968.)

It will already have become apparent that these discoveries raise new and formidable difficulties for the psycho-physical identity theory. It postulates that conscious experiences run parallel with the brain events, and for each brain event there is a unique conscious experience. Moreover, the association is postulated to be automatic, requiring no mechanism of interaction. Parallelism thus gives a simple and attractive explanation of perceptual experiences but denies that consciousness can exert any effective action on neural happenings.

Of course, it is always open to the identity theorist to assert that whenever a conscious experience occurs, a new and unique physical pattern must have been produced before the experience could happen to the subject. And indeed, it is impossible with our present knowledge to give a categorical denial of this—and perhaps it always will be impossible. But the impact of work such as Sperry's does seem to make such a theory highly implausible, if not incredible, so the burden of proof must remain with the identity theorist.

A fundamental neurological problem is: how can the 'willing' of a muscular movement set in train neural events which lead to the discharge of the pyramidal cells of the motor cortex, and so activate the neural pathway which leads to muscular contraction? We are all convinced, and rightly so, that by thinking and willing we can control our actions if we so wish, although in normal waking life this prerogative is exercised but seldom. As the famous neuro-surgeon, Wilder Penfield, discovered many years ago, electrical stimulation of the motor cortex of conscious subjects evokes actions which are disowned by the subject. As he says, 'When a subject observes such an action he remarks, "That was due to something done to me and not done by me." ' From this it follows that a motor action emanating from the motor cortex in response to a voluntary command has some concomitants which are lacking when a similar motor action is elicited by artificial stimulation of the motor cortex. In 1969 a group of workers detected, at various sites on the surface of the skull, a slowly rising negative potential in the brain cells, called 'readiness potential', two seconds before a subject starts to do something entirely on his own volition. The whole cerebral surface is affected by this readiness potential, except for certain areas of the most anterior and basal regions. Usually such a readiness potential begins about 850 milliseconds before the onset of the movement and in its turn leads to sharper potentials, negative or positive, less than 100 milliseconds before the movement. These sharper potentials are located more specifically over those areas of the motor cortex which are to be concerned with the movement. Eccles says, 'We can assume that the "readiness potential" is generated by complex patterned neuronal discharges that eventually project to the pyramidal cells of the motor cortex and synaptically excite them to discharge, so generating the waves just preceding the movement.'

There have been some challenging suggestions as to how the onset of a readiness potential might be developed through the postulated action of the will on a few neurons or even on a single neuron, and through detection by other 'critically poised'

neurons, spread through the brain tissue, to produce the deflec-
tion of spatio-temporal pattern which must occur before the
action actually reaches performance. This is too technical to
warrant our following it through here. It is, however, worth
quoting Sperry's conclusion on this matter of mind and brain as
a result primarily of his long period of study of split-brain
patients.

He postulates that the conscious phenomena of subjective
experience do interact on the brain processes, exerting an active
causal influence. In this view, consciousness is conceived to have
a directive role in determining the flow pattern of cerebral excitation. Conscious phenomena in his scheme are conceived to
interact with and largely to govern the physicochemical and
physiological aspects of the brain process. He continues,

It obviously works the other way round as well, and thus a mutual
interaction is conceived between the physiological and the mental
properties. Even so, the present interpretation would tend to restore
mind to its old prestigious position over matter, in the sense that the
mental phenomena are seen to transcend the phenomena of physiology and biochemistry. . . . *Consciousness does do things and is highly
functional as an important component of the causal sequence in higher
level reactions. This is a view that puts consciousness to work. It gives
the phenomena of consciousness a use and a reason for being and for
having been evolved.* [My italics. W.H.T.]

The discovery mentioned above that the mechanisms necessary for this association of consciousness with the dominant
hemisphere are already being laid down in the early foetus,
whereas no comparable cerebral asymmetry has been found in
chimpanzees, gives rise to many questions. We have seen that
these animals have the ability to learn and use sign language
effectively; and we have also seen that, in spite of the preformed
asymmetry in the human brain in regard to the development of
the speech area, this does not mean that these areas are the only
parts of the brain that control speech. So we seem to be forced to
the conclusion that the fact that both speech and consciousness
are typically concentrated in the same particular area of the
brain in nearly all normal human beings must certainly have
been a recent development which took place in the early stages of
the evolution of the genus *Homo* as we know it. The probable
explanation is that the verbal-linguistic development in evolu-

tion made immense demands on neuronal resources and that it was as a result of this that the specialization of the two hemispheres in different directions was initiated. As Eccles says, 'One can imagine that progressively more subtle linguistic performance gave primitive man the opportunities for very effective survival, which may be regarded as a strong evolutionary pressure. As a consequence there were the marvellously rapid evolutionary changes transforming, in two to three million years, a primitive ape to the present human race.'

The dualism of matter and mind as seen by philosophers and physiologists

The universal, or almost universal, reaction to the dualism of Descartes has, in the past century or so, led to an overwhelming preference by most scientific people for physical explanations, for the very good reason that the adoption of such theories has made, and is making, possible vast progress in the field of science. But recently there has been an increasing tendency for those scientists who have any philosophical understanding at all, and in particular those who have any comprehension of the problems of epistemology (of the nature of knowledge and of knowing), to change their views on this. Here it is appropriate to discuss the recent papers of a very distinguished scientific philosopher, Sir Karl Popper (1968a, b), who comes down on the side of dualism.[1] He sees that no explanation of the physical world can be valid which regards the self-consciousness of man as being merely an epiphenomenon—an accidental outcome of the mechanical workings of a machine which we call the brain. That is, there must be in fact two worlds—the world of consciousness, of self-knowing, and the physical world which is known by the operations of the scientific method. And of course the scientific method can be carried out only by a 'knowing' being.

Popper's three-world theory

Popper's recent papers amount to something more—to a 'three-world plan', and this three-world plan has fairly recently (1970) been developed or elaborated, from the neurophysiological point of view. (See Table 7 and Figs. 12 & 13 pp. 96–8.) Of Popper's

1. For another modern philosophy of dualism, see A. C. Ewing, *Value and reality: the philosophical case for theism*, Allen & Unwin, London, 1973.

Table 7
Popper's three worlds
(From Eccles, 1970.)

World 1 Physical objects and states	World 2 States of consciousness	World 3 Knowledge in objective sense

1. Inorganic
Matter and energy
of cosmos
	Subjective knowledge
	
	Experience of:
	  perception,
		1. Record of intellectual efforts:
		  philosophical,
		  theological,

2. Biology Structure and actions of all living beings, human brains	thinking, emotions, dispositional intentions, memories, dreams,	scientific, historical, literary, artistic, technological

3. Artifacts
Material substrates
of human creativity:
  tools,
  machines,
  books,
  works of art,
  music
	creative
	  imagination
		2. Theoretical
		systems:
		  scientific
		    problems,
		  critical
		    arguments

three worlds the first is the world of physical objects and states. As such, this 'World I' comprises not only inorganic matter and the energy of the cosmos but also all biology: the structures and actions of the bodies of all living beings—plants and animals and even human brains. It also comprises the material substratum of all man-made objects or artifacts: machines, books, works of art, films, and computers. The second world is the world of states of consciousness or of mental states. (Here we are for the time being dealing solely with human consciousness, but I shall have something to say later about the evidence for animal consciousness.) 'World 2' is thus the world that each of us knows at first hand only for himself and for others by inference. It is the world of knowledge in the subjective sense and comprises the ongoing experiences of perception, of thinking, of emotions, of

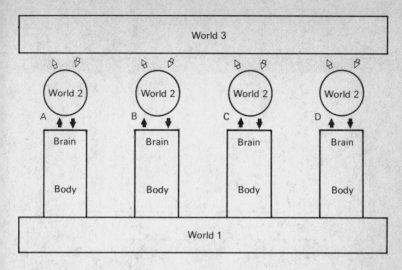

Fig. 12: Information-flow showing interaction between Worlds 1, 2, and 3 for four individuals. World 3 is represented as being 'impressed' on a special part of World 1 (books, pictures, films, tapes, etc.) that forms an indefinitely extending layer. It is to be understood that any individual is able to move into relationship with any particular part of World 3 that is of interest to him. (From Eccles, 1974, after Eccles, 1970.)

imaginings, of dispositional intentions, and of memories. By contrast there is another world, and it is here that I think philosophers may look askance at Popper's conclusions. 'World 3', the world of knowledge in the objective sense, has an extremely wide range of contents. For example, it comprises the expressions of scientific, literary, and artistic thoughts codified in libraries and museums and all the records of human culture. Material compositions, paper and ink, are of course in 'World 1', but the knowledge conveyed by these artifacts is in 'World 3'. According to Popper, the most important components of 'World 3' are the theoretical systems comprising scientific problems and the critical arguments generated by the discussion of these problems. So 'World 3' comprises the records of the intellectual efforts of mankind through all ages up to the present—the cultural heritage of mankind. This view will perhaps be made clearer in Fig. 13. In order to illustrate the independent existence

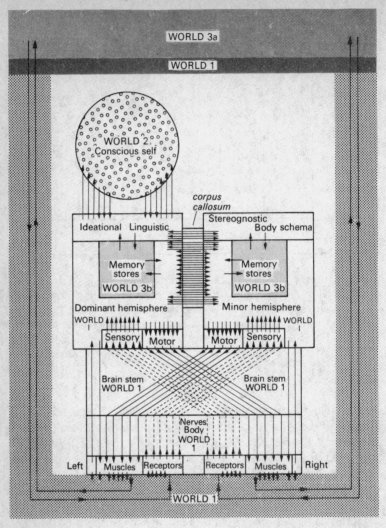

Fig. 13: Communications to and from the brain and within the brain. The diagram shows the principal lines of communication from peripheral receptors to the sensory cortices and so to the cerebral hemispheres. Similarly, the diagram shows the output from the cerebral hemispheres via the motor cortex and so to muscles. Both these systems of pathways are largely crossed as illustrated, but minor uncrossed pathways are also shown. The dominant left hemisphere and minor right hemisphere are labelled, together with some of the properties of these hemispheres that are found displayed in Fig. 9.

of this third world, Popper suggests two 'thought experiments':

Experiment One. Imagine that all our machines and tools are destroyed, and also all our subjective learning, including our subjective knowledge of machines and tools and how to use them. But libraries and our capacity to learn from them survive. In theory, after much suffering, our world may get going again.

Experiment Two. As before, machines and tools and our subjective learning are destroyed, including our subjective knowledge of machines and tools and how to use them. But this time, all libraries are destroyed also, so that our capacity to learn from books becomes useless.

As Popper says, if we think about these two experiments, the reality, the significance, and the degree of autonomy of the 'third' world (as well as its effects on the 'second' and 'first' worlds) may perhaps become a little clearer. For in the second case there will be no re-emergence of our civilization for many millennia. As Eccles says, if we think of the history of the human race, we note that in Experiment Two man would be transported far back into prehistory and would have to begin again the long upward climb that characterized the tens of thousands of years from Neanderthal man, through Cro-Magnon man, and so eventually to the epochs of history. Even the great destruction of the Roman Empire was incomplete, for there were islands of culture with written records that survived, and eventually the recovery of classical literature came partly through the isolated monastic centres and the scholars of the Arab world. We must realize that knowledge in the objective sense is a product of human intellectual activity and, although it has an existence independent of a knowing subject, it must be potentially capable of being known. That is to say, though it is largely autonomous, it is not absolutely and finally autonomous. A similar example is provided by the Linear B scripts of the Minoan civilization so brilliantly deciphered by Michael Ventris. The information symbolically carried by the scripts was nevertheless in 'World 3' because they were potentially capable of being deciphered.

Fig. 13 (cont.): The *corpus callosum* is shown as a powerful cross linking of the two hemispheres and, in addition, the diagram displays the modes of interaction between Worlds 1, 2, and 3, as described in the text. (From Eccles, 1974.)

Popper's discussion of Worlds 2 and 3 suggests that:

... a subjective mental world of personal experience exists (a thesis denied by the behaviourist) ... and that it is one of the main functions of the 'second world' to grasp the objects of the 'third world'. This is something we all do; it is part of being human to learn a language; and this means, essentially, to learn to grasp *objective thought contents* ... so that one day we will have to revolutionise psychology by looking at the human mind as primarily an organ for interacting with the objects of the 'third world'; for understanding them, contributing to them, participating in them; and for bringing them to bear on the 'first world'.

This is only, of course, the baldest résumé of an important theory. But one additional comment may be helpful here. It is that since the objects in 'World 1'—the natural world, the world of physical objects and states—can, as is obvious, be interpreted, understood, and, if you like, 'translated' by the activities of organized science, then does it not follow that the physical world which can be so understood and translated is in a sense on a par with Popper's 'World 3'? It is a world which has been understood, to a very, very small extent, by the proved experience of scientific man during the last ten thousand years, and therefore this understanding is of course in 'World 3'. Can it not be plausibly argued that what man is understanding is in fact a 'pre-existing' knowledge of nature, a plan which ties the whole universe together in a creative unity; and further, that it is this, which by such laborious and painful processes, we may partly come to understand? If this is so, all the evidences for the understanding of this plan would lie also in the 'third world'. As Eccles points out, this suggests Plato's world of forms and ideas; but is not Popper's thought quite different? For Plato the third world comprised eternal verities that provided ultimate explanations and meanings for all our experiences, and our efforts were concerned only with trying to grasp and understand these eternal verities. This was a transcendental world, a world of possible objects of thought. Popper's point is that his third world is man-made and arises from our efforts to understand and make intelligible 'World 1' and even 'World 2'. His is the world of civilization and cultures from all ages to the present. But if, as I hope I have shown above, there is some real evidence for consciousness in subhuman types and that there is also evidence for at least the beginnings of culture (in the sense of a transmitted body of knowledge) amongst animals, then perhaps Popper's world will begin to look slightly different.

Philosophical reductionism and Gödel's theory
Popper (1972) believes philosophical reductionism is a mistake, arising from the wish to reduce everything to an ultimate explanation in terms of essences and substances—an explanation which is incapable of any further explanation. We can of course go on asking the question 'Why?', but 'Why' questions never lead to an ultimate answer. Popper comes to the conclusion that it is the very nature of science itself to be essentially incomplete, a point of view stressed many years ago by Professor Herbert Dingle and others.

But there is, as Popper says, a further reason why any explanatory science cannot be completed, for to be complete it would have to give an explanatory account of itself. A further result is implicit in Gödel's famous theorem of the 'incompletability' of formalized arithmetics. Since all physical science uses arithmetic (and since for a reductionist only science formulated in physical symbols has any reality), Gödel's incompleteness theory renders all physical science incomplete, which to the reductionist should show that all science is incomplete. As Popper puts it, 'For the non-reductionist, who does not believe in the reducibility of all science to physically formulated science, science is incomplete anyway.' Not only is philosophical reductionism a mistake, but the belief that the method of reduction can achieve complete reductions is, Popper believes, mistaken too. We live, so it appears, in a world of emergent evolution, and of problems whose solutions, if they are solved, beget new and deeper problems. Thus we live in a universe of emergent novelty —a novelty which is seldom completely reducible to any of the preceding stages. As Marjorie Grene (1966) says, we can never prove the consistency of the whole, for it is always open-ended: 'This is a formal admission which is philosophically of the highest importance.'

References

This chapter is largely a summary and condensation of Ch. 9 of:
Thorpe, W. H. (1974) *Animal nature and human nature*, Methuen, London, and Doubleday-Anchor, New York.
Many of the detailed references will be found there. Other general

texts which will be found useful as further reading for this chapter and will supply details of many other sources are:

Ayala, F. J., and Dobzhansky, T. (eds.) (1974) *Studies in the philosophy of biology*, Macmillan, London. (See especially Ch. 7.)

Dubos, R. J. (1951) *Louis Pasteur: freelance of science*, Gollancz, London.

Eccles, J. C. (ed.) (1966) *Brain and conscious experience*, Springer, Berlin, Heidelberg, and New York.

────── (1970) *Facing reality*, Springer, Berlin, Heidelberg, and New York.

Griffin, D. R. (1976) *The problem of animal awareness*, Rockefeller University Press, New York.

Koestler, A. (1967) *The ghost in the machine*, Hutchinson, London.

Pantin, C. F. A. (1968) *The relation between the sciences* (edited with introduction and notes by A. M. Pantin and W. H. Thorpe), Cambridge University Press, Cambridge and London.

Popper, K. (1968) 'On the theory of the objective mind', *Akten des XIV Internat. Kongr. f. Philosophie*, Vol. 1, Herder, Wien.

────── (1972) *Objective knowledge: an evolutionary approach*, Clarendon Press, Oxford.

Sherrington, C. S. (1940) *Man on his nature*, Cambridge University Press, Cambridge and London.

Thorpe, W. H. (1963) *Learning and instinct in animals*, 2nd edn., Methuen, London, and Harvard University Press, Cambridge, Mass., and New York.

5
The primacy of 'mind' in nature

In the first chapter I referred to the revolution in scientific thought which occurred at the turn of the century. There we saw that physicists fully accepted the disappearance of the idea that mechanism was, in some way, the basis of the physical world. No longer were they tempted to believe that ultimate reality could ever be 'explained' by concepts of the concrete. Of course, the ordinary mechanical concepts were as valuable as ever for dealing with macrophysics, the behaviour of matter *en masse*. Similarly, for the greater part of the living world, where we are dealing with matter on the macro, rather than the micro, scale, mechanical explanations seemed to become more and more attractive the more carefully the structures and adaptations of animals were discussed and described. So it is that though the basic world of the physicist (with its 'Quarks', 'Charm', 'strangeness', and other concepts) is even more insubstantial and mysterious and further removed from mechanism than before, the world of living things became after the 1920s ever more a world of mechanical models, of chemical and physical models, of causality, and of mechanism. Thus it was not until biologists were beginning to appreciate the fact that mental phenomena, which are seen to be only partially explicable in terms of the mechanical, might be playing an important role at various stages in the story of evolution—particularly in the study of the evolution of the higher animals—that this tendency of biologists to emphasize the mechanical began to be doubted. And indeed the very completeness and effectiveness of the developments in molecular biology and genetics began to illuminate, in their turn, the fact that there were still large unresolved problems of breathtaking difficulty involved in biological studies. (See Lewontin, 1974.)

Whitehead's 'Process Philosophy'

There was one philosopher-metaphysician of the time who was unique in his grasp of the mathematical principles underlying the new physics and yet who in his other writings displayed a profound and shrewd understanding of the current developments in biology. This was Alfred North Whitehead. As a mathematician and logician his position was secured by his mighty work with Bertrand Russell, *Principia Mathematica*. This attempted to establish mathematics as the basis for a reformed formal logic. I believe that it indeed was, as has so often been claimed, one of the great intellectual monuments of all time.

To those biologists of my generation who were prepared to look beyond the immediate techniques and problems of their science, and who began to see that a basic metaphysic (as fully worked out as possible) is essential to the healthy progress of science, if not to its very existence, Whitehead as a philosopher was the great figure to whom we looked. This was partly because we felt that no other philosopher had written so understandingly and profoundly of what were essentially biological problems. But beyond all this there was his most profound and important book, namely *Process and Reality* (1929). Not many of us biologists really got very far with this—a metaphysical work of great length, profundity, and complexity of detail; indeed, as one commentator has put it, a work of monumental opacity. But it is abundantly clear now that this work is as great in its way as *Principia Mathematica*, and that Whitehead shows himself to be one of the greatest of Western metaphysicians and, above all, the metaphysician who was without a rival in his understanding of biology in the modern developments of his time. For all of us who were not professional philosophers, and for many who were, this immense masterpiece needed, and still needs, professional exegesis and interpretation.

So it was that the coming of the logical positivists, to whom nothing was more anathema than Whitehead's kind of metaphysics, ensured that Whitehead's philosophy of science was, for the time being, effectively buried. I remember on one occasion asking the late Professor Gilbert Ryle to remind me of the title of his chair at Oxford. He replied, with a look of extreme distaste, 'Metaphysical Philosophy—whatever that may mean!' This was by no means a unique indication of the cast of mind of the dominant schools of philosophy in the 1940s and 1950s. It was this bias which led to the attack on the customary distinction made between physical and mental events, by calling the latter 'the ghost in the machine'.

The professional bias which led to the temporary neglect of Whitehead's metaphysics did not, however, by any means outlaw the more popular works; and whatever the philosophical climate of the time, *Science and the Modern World* (1925), *Adventures of Ideas* (1933), *Modes of Thought* (1938), and *Religion in the Making* (1920) continued to have a wide readership. This was perhaps more because of their profound wit and wisdom and the scintillating effect of the author's wide reading and erudition, classical and modern, than because of any general acceptance of his philosophical position or indeed any wide understanding of it.

Now, however, following the enormous progress of biological science, together with a wide appreciation of the basic fatuity of the original logical-positivist position, Whitehead's importance is coming to be more than ever appreciated. It is a curious fact that, as Marjorie Grene has pointed out, the reason why the early logical positivism was doomed was that, as in Wittgenstein's *Tractatus*, logic and the wholly precise speech of logically governed science could mirror the universe only if the universe were composed solely of atomic facts. But these fundamental atomic facts are nowhere to be found; nor are there any atomic sentences with which to begin such a construction. If we can speak only exactly, by using an aggregate of wholly precise atomic statements to build our discourse, and if of all that is not thus exactly articulated we must remain silent, then we must be silent altogether! For all discourse, even that which has led to such a conclusion, becomes absurd. We are left only with what Wittgenstein calls the 'ethical' and 'mystical', about which speech is impossible. Wittgenstein himself recognized such problems and strove, during the remainder of his life, to overcome them.

What Whitehead did was to take 'time' seriously and to provide a conceptual framework ready to hand, which, as Marjorie Grene says, 'was truly founded on the priority of Process'. So it is that Whitehead's philosophy seems to be coming into its own. Therefore it is highly desirable to look carefully at the Whiteheadian system anew in order to determine its significance for our day. But though what I have just said suggests that I am optimistic about the change of view and of emphasis which we have seen recently, we must never forget that mechanism rules in its proper sphere and that the mechanistic world-picture remains (in spite of its inherent philosophical confusions) highly attractive to most scientists as a world view and still, even now, provides a formidable opposition to any other.

The mechanistic world-picture sees the universe as a machine or contrivance, and all that is in it as smaller machines or contrivances which, once set in motion, perform as they do by virtue of their construction. This idea, having originated in the physical sciences, was, as we have seen, taken over by the biologists even while being relinquished as the fundamental basis of physics; and it greatly aided the practical development and establishment of biology as a universally recognized scientific system. Since the assumption that living beings are mechanisms based on physics is, at intermediate levels and in large measure, obviously true and has yielded (and is continuing to yield) such immense practical dividends, it is hardly suprising that it is still, in many quarters, regarded as the sole biological orthodoxy.

Yet, as long ago as 1926, Whitehead said, 'It is orthodox to hold that there is nothing in biology other than what is physical mechanism under somewhat complex circumstances. . . . The appeal to mechanism on behalf of biology was, in its origin, an appeal to the well-attested self-consistent physical concepts as expressing the basis of all natural phenomena; but at present there is no such system of concepts.' And as Birch (1974) points out, the trouble with mechanical determinism is that it does not work—principally because there is nothing ultimate about the physicists' atoms and molecules. This orthodoxy incorporates two attitudes which are radically inconsistent. Again, Whitehead says (1926), 'A scientific realism based on mechanism is conjoined with an unwavering belief in the world of men and the higher animals as being composed of self-determining organisms.' The great difficulty is to get from one to the other, and in this connection Whitehead remarks, 'A thoroughgoing evolutionary philosophy is inconsistent with materialism; the aboriginal stuff or material from which materialistic philosophy starts, is incapable of evolution. . . .'

Whitehead was trying to establish a philosophy of organism which could include both physics and biology. He achieved this by regarding 'process' as primary to both; and this involved postulating a 'mental pole' as well as a 'physical pole' from the beginning. He thus reverses the situation of the mechanists by saying that we do not start by knowing all about atoms and molecules and then seek to understand the phenomena of biology. It is from the observed phenomena in biology that we have to start with 'occasions of experiences'. From these we should work back to construct models of similar entities. Moreover, atoms that can give rise to brains that think must be different from hypothetical atoms which under no circumstances could have done this. To put it in another way, the evolution of the subjective is the crux of our problem. The historical processes of life have given rise to ourselves who know the existence of a subjective aspect of life in our own lives. This subjective aspect is obviously a central fact of our existence. If we ask, 'Where in evolution did the subjective start?' it becomes extremely attractive to give the answer, 'It was everywhere and must have been a part of everything.' Thus we find Whitehead talking about 'subjective aim' as part of the fundamental nature of things and analogous to 'purpose' at the human level, and as the anticipation of the future and therefore of the influence of the future on the present. This brings us to the view that what we call 'things' are not really 'things' but events. For him Reality is Process. An entity, as it is to itself, is a subject; but as it appears to us is an object. From this, Whitehead leads on to one of the most fundamental elements of his beliefs, namely that subjective aim is postulated because, without it, no entity could even exist. Al entities are processes. (That, incidentally, is essentially what modern physical theory is saying: all entities are processes, and there is no 'thing' in the universe.) Moreover, the theory of subjective aim tells us that unless subjective aims existed in entities, no organisms could have ever come into existence. I agree with Charles Birch when he says, 'It seems to me therefore that the metaphysical background of process thought is far more germane to the evolutionary picture provided by biology than is the mechanistic philosophy, explicit or implicit, which so often accompanies evolutionary theory.'

Following these conclusions, which as we have seen were derived from the revelation reached by the state of theoretical physics, in this new and totally surprising epoch of science, Whitehead had to build a metaphysic around the nature of the non-mechanical entities the behaviour of which was being described by the equations of the theoretical physicists. Since, quite clearly, the universe was not random in anything like the formal sense of that word, he could only assume that these unknowable events, or processes, which were behind and at the basis of the physicists' equations, were in some way directed or purposeful. As R. H. Overman pointed out, one of the great problems of modern scientific thought has been that people have been sure that, somehow or other, everything depends on purposes somewhere, in something or other—but they have hardly ever had any very clear grasp of just where the purposes are, in what things, and to what extent. 'So sometimes they have rendered to God the purposes that really were Caesar's,' and sometimes they have credited crowds of Caesar's cells—liver cells, bone-marrow cells, blood-cells, or whatever—with a unified conscious vision, a vision which of course only Caesar's soul could have enjoyed. Everyone knows the result of this muddle, which was the gradual elimination of the notion of purpose from scientific thought. Overman claims that, in a very odd way, it also disappeared from theological thought; but this can be doubted.

In order to get out of such muddles, Whitehead directs our attention away from large-scale enduring things to what he calls 'occasions of experience', which are short-lived entities whose subjective aims determine their becoming. Thus all the activities of the basic unknowable elements of the cosmos must first be regarded as subjective aims of short-lived entities. It is these subjective aims which determine their becoming. These aims, being purely subjective, are entirely private and can become known to us in any way only through their becoming, by which they become possible objects of thought. But in thinking of the world we cannot conceive the directionality of these basic individual occasions. Instead we are conscious of and think almost entirely of groups or 'nexuses' of entities arranged in some complex temporal and spatial pattern. Whitehead calls any such group of occasions with some sort of connectedness, a 'nexus'; and a nexus which shows some trait shared by each member in dependence on the others he calls a society.

For example, what we usually call an 'electron' is a 'society of occasions', each a distinct process of becoming, each extremely short-lived, each inheriting some characteristic feelings (which we call electronic) from a predecessor and mediating them to a successor. Taken as a whole such a society, stretching through time, is an enduring object. So a 'molecule' is an 'enduring object', a temporally ordered society of molecular occasions containing sub-societies of atoms. Ordinary things of experience, such as rocks and tables, are composed of many strands of enduring objects, and the story of planetary evolution focuses on the careers of incredibly complex organisms which may be analysed into societies with sub-societies of many kinds. But even the most complex order of life can be analysed ultimately into the relationships among short-lived occasions with subjective aims. Whitehead insists that the reasons for things always lie in actual entities, and since all of these are remote from our comprehension it is no wonder that we often speak confusedly.

Everyone would agree that a moment of human experience is richer, more intense, more laden with intrinsic value than is a moment of electronic experience, and that this complex human experience has gradually evolved from simpler kinds of entities. Whitehead thus sees the 'problems' faced by nature as having two aspects—evolution had to produce complex societies if the earth were to flourish with actual occasions which, individually, enjoy greater intensities of experiences. Whatever the level of complexity in the occasions of a society, the society only 'counts' in evolution if it has a method of surviving. Whitehead sees two ways in which nature has solved this problem of survival.

1. Material bodies such as rocks and stars are composed of societies of·occasions. But we must assume that there is, so to speak, a 'mental pole' in these occasions which operates only at a trivial level. Such societies are what we call inorganic, and we correctly recognize them as being dominated by the patterns of physical feeling which stimulate our sense-organs and scientific instruments. As has already been said, each occasion is first a subject whose process of becoming is absolutely private, and then afterwards an object which can have an effect upon subsequent subjects. What Whitehead calls the physical purposes of such occasions are dominant, so in practice we can afford to disregard all questions other than the physical characteristics of such enduring objects.

2. The second way for societies of occasions to survive is by changing their defining characteristics somewhat, by admitting novelty in the form of conceptual feelings—as Whitehead puts it, 'The world advances into novelty along a road paved with

propositions.' (Overman, p. 7.) A proposition of this kind is entertained by the mentality of an occasion as a possibility of becoming something more than would be implied if it were merely to conform to past matter of fact. For this to succeed, the 'something more' must be a quality of feeling which can be reconciled with the already existing characteristics of the society. Whitehead regards these as the basic examples of 'adaptation to the environment' directed by final causation; and societies in which this method of survival is important are what he calls 'living societies'. In this sense, then, life is the escape from physical routine. But he also insists that in the lowest grade of living societies, this purposive adaptation occurs entirely without any consciousness; all that is required is that an occasion be able to incorporate some alternative for itself beyond what is supplied by physical feelings of its past.

In Overman's words,

The overall picture, then, is one of life on earth as a passage from mere physical order to mental novelty, and from mental novelty to coordinated inheritance of mental novelty. If in this way we can trace the 'upward thrust' of evolution to the subjective aims of actual occasions, *locating final causation in nature*, the time-honoured expression 'natural selection' can be used easily in a broadened sense: evolution towards 'adaptation' to the environment involves the survival of societies whose occasions aim to incorporate within a richer experience influences which might otherwise be destructive.

There are four discernible kinds of actual occasions listed by Whitehead:

1. Occasions in empty space which we cannot detect by sensory means.

2. Occasions in inorganic enduring objects (e.g., electrons, rock molecules).

3. Occasions in enduring living objects, enjoying a degree of conceptual novelty.

4. Occasions in the life-histories of living persons with conscious knowledge.

There are also four kinds of aggregates of occasion on earth:

1. Inorganic things which persist for long periods.

2. Vegetable-grade things, complex 'democracies of cells' whose occasions seem to have no aims beyond survival.

3. Animal-grade things, where some occasions, at least, seem

to enjoy aims for experience richer than necessary for mere survival.

4. Human life, with its immense powers of novel conceptuality.

Mysterious though this metaphysics of Whitehead may seem at first to the scientists, I think we can understand how it was he came to these views and conceive something of the brilliance of thought which enabled him to achieve this extraordinarily powerful system. Being so acutely conscious of the fact that the new physics left no room for static 'matter', but appeared rather to be all an affair of changing relationships between non-mechanical entities, he came to the unavoidable conclusion that process must be the key to further understanding; and that therefore all reality is basically 'flow and movement: never static and constant'. Hence he came to the view that since the basic stuff of the world could not be regarded as physical, it was nearer to sense to regard it as mental—since there was no other term (with the possible exception of 'spiritual') that could meet the need. So he arrived at 'occasions of experience' and produced major revolutions in both metaphysics and epistemology. The first of these revolutions was that of 'occasions of experience'; the second, of creativity, which involved the 'many' becoming 'one'. The revolution in epistemology was that 'mental' equalled the element of novelty (the novel pole) and that 'physical' equalled the repetitious pole. The implication of this is that the mental element in the physical pole can be almost completely ignored—though not entirely ignored, because without it we cannot conceive of physical existence at all, for any type of entity.

It will at once appear that Whitehead's system is not dualistic but monistic in that it is concerned with 'actual entities' as vital, transient occasions of experience, basic to the whole cosmos. In this sense at least the mental is primary in Whitehead's thought. But this of course does not rule out the very practical kind of dualism which Karl Popper has set forth so illuminatingly, as bound up with the mental powers of human beings.

Purposes in physics and biology

As this book has emphasized, from the philosophical point of view the central problem of ethology is the relation between purposiveness ('purpose' here has the usual meaning—a striving after a future goal retained as some kind of an image or idea) and directiveness. All biologists agree that the behaviour of organisms as a whole is directive, in the sense that in the course of evolution at least some of it has been modified by selection so as to lead with greater or less certainty towards states which favour the survival and reproduction of the individual. All machines are also directive in the sense that their parts have been designed or selected so as to behave in a particular way whenever activated by an external source of power; but not even the most elaborate machine, such as a computer, is purposive. So for the ethologist the question is, 'How much, if any, of the animal's behaviour is purposive, and what is the relation of this behaviour to the rest?'

This, to me, ties up in a very important way with our consideration of a living animal as primarily something which perceives. In human perception, as H. H. Price (1932) shows, the very idea of a material object is dependent upon an element of anticipation. He says, 'Every perceptual act anticipates its own confirmation by subsequent acts.' Whitehead (1929) considers the act of perception as the establishment by the subject of its causal relation with its own external world at a particular moment. He argues that every vital event in fact involves a process of the type which, when we are distinguishing between mental and material, we describe as mental—the act of perception. A very strong case is made by Agar (1943) for the theory that a living organism is essentially something which perceives. Therefore, some element of anticipation and memory, in other words some essential ability to deal with events in time as in space, is, by definition, to be expected throughout the world of living things.

All this, so far as it goes, fits in well with modern Whiteheadian conceptions. But this is not to say that the metaphysics of Whitehead is of much help as a guide for the research biologist, except in so far as it encourages him, first, to concentrate on the key problem of perceptual synthesis, and, secondly, to doubt the reliability of Lloyd Morgan's 'canon' as the sole guide to research at the present day. These are, admittedly, very important matters, and my own desire to investigate the 'higher' and more complex aspects of animal behaviour, and not to rest content with Lloyd Morgan's injunction, may well have been due to my early reading of Whitehead. Lloyd Morgan's 'canon' insists that one should never adopt a complex theory or formulation for a given behaviour when a 'simpler' (usually a more 'mechanical' or more physiological) one would suffice. It was a most valuable warning at a time when, following Romanes and other naturalists of the period, strongly anthropocentric attitudes were absurdly rampant. Nowadays, the study of perceptual synthesis, of memory, of ideation, of insightful problem-solving, and of the complexities of motivation in animals, has reached a point at which the exact opposite of Morgan's strategy often seems more promising.

For myself I nevertheless find (as implied above) the discontinuities in nature so great and so obvious that I stick to the dualist position as an essential attitude of mind—I am, so to speak, a pragmatic dualist. But I can say with certainty that the only type of monism I can envisage as in any sense acceptable is one of the Whiteheadian type. In this respect, and perhaps in others, Whitehead's system does have some special illumination of value to biologists; for adherence to the rule of Lloyd Morgan's canon, from its being a most valuable guide to the nineteenth century, has come to be a real hindrance and stumbling-block to biologists in the later twentieth century.

The mental primary to the physical
To sum up in brief the most important features, from our point of view, of the Whiteheadian doctrine, I think one should re-iterate two things. First, the ultimate physical entities of science are always vectors indicating transference (Whitehead, 1929, p. 364). This is another way of saying that 'being' is 'becoming'. Whitehead himself (1929, p. 571) translates Heraclitus' saying, 'All things flow,' as 'All things are vectors.' And finally although, as we have said, the mental pole can mainly be ignored when we are dealing with purely physical matters, 'Even the physical world cannot be understood without reference to a complex of mental operations.' (1929, p. 366.)

At this point I should like to quote, with permission, two statements on the scientific significance of Whitehead's views by two participants in a recent (1974) conference entitled 'Mind in Nature' (Cobb and Griffin, 1977). Sewell Wright, one of the supreme pioneers of the modern selectionist theory of evolution, says,

My final conclusion is that there is real satisfaction in a philosophy which can bring under a common viewpoint the vast body of secondary but verifiable knowledge of the external world which constitutes

science, with its necessarily deterministic and probabilistic inter-
pretations, and the primary but private knowledge which each of us
has of his own stream of consciousness, more or less continually
directed towards the finding of an acceptable course through the
difficulties of the external world by means of voluntary actions.

Charles Hartshorne, one of the most outstanding living ex-
ponents of Whitehead's system, says,

On this view 'mind' is not confined to a corner of nature but is everywhere in it, just as behaviour is. But mind is the substance, and mere
behaviour, spatio-temporal change, is the shadow, the skeletal outline only, the causal geometry of nature.

In a contribution to the same conference Arthur Koestler
discusses 'Free will in a hierarchic context'—the context being
the hierarchic organization of all living beings. He points out the
very well known fact, that a skill practised and repeated in a
monotonous environment, in the absence of novelty, tends to
degenerate into a mechanical routine. Confrontation with any
unexpected or challenging situation, however, such as the immediate prospect of a collision for someone driving a car, poses
new problems which must be referred to a higher level in the
hierarchy, and in such a case will cause a shift from purely
'mechanical' to fully conscious or 'mindful' behaviour. Such
sudden upward shifts from mechanical routine towards original-
ity and improvization are well known to ethologists in widely
different phyla of the animal kingdom.

Koestler looks upon these as precursors of the phenomena of
human creativity which point to the existence of unsuspected
potential in the organism, which are dormant in the normal
routines of existence but may emerge in response to new challenges offered by the environment.

Returning to man and his everyday behaviour, he discusses
the development of an intention in ourselves, whether it is the
expression of an idea or just the lighting of a cigarette, as a
process of triggering patterns of sub-routines into action, a
'particularisation of a general intent'. On the other hand, the
referring of decisions to higher levels is an integrative process
which tends to establish a higher degree of co-ordination and
wholeness of experience. Thus, every upward shift would represent a quasi-holistic move, every downward shift a particular-
izing move, 'the former characterised by heightened awareness

and mentalistic attributes, the latter by diminishing awareness and mechanistic attributes'. As we ascend in the hierarchy, we hand over decisions to higher echelons and in so doing have the experience of free choice. But, he argues (I am sure correctly), this is not merely a subjective experience, for at each step upward the constraints of the lower levels decrease and the number of possible choices increases. But our belief in free will as an absolutely general category, which we have discussed above, implies that the hierarchy, as we go up towards an ever greater freedom of choice, is open-ended, towards an infinite regress, without ever reaching a ceiling. The higher the level to which the decision is referred the less predictable the choice. If we assume that the ultimate decision rests with the apex of the hierarchy, we delude ourselves; for the apex itself is not at rest, it keeps receding. 'The self which has the ultimate responsibility for a man's actions, eludes the grasp of its own awareness.'

The materialist scientist of the last century, looking downward into the basis of material things, thought that he found material entities behaving according to mechanistic determinism in a lawful and invariable manner to constitute the material world. At the other end he had the curious illusion that his mentality was also determined by mechanistic-materialist laws.

Now, as we have seen, materialism at the basic physical levels has been transformed into events involving entities which are certainly not 'physical' in any original sense but as 'vectors' to be described only in non-physical terms—as 'mental', as 'purposive', or as 'spiritual'. Again, if we climb upwards towards the top of the hierarchy and try to understand the human mind with its freedom of the will, we find the universe dissolving into an infinity of mind which is, and can only be, the sole way of understanding 'the universe'.

As Arthur Koestler puts it, 'Man is neither a plaything of the gods nor a marionette suspended on its chromosomes.' However much philosophers may dislike the concept of infinite regress, we cannot get away from the infinite; for the infinity of mind seems to encompass us everywhere. 'Infinity stares us in the face, whether we look at the stars or search for our own identities. A true science of life must let infinity in and never lose sight of it.' (See also Pasteur, quoted p. 79 above.)

The use of the word 'infinity' here and in the quotation from Pasteur may seem somewhat puzzling; so some comment appears desirable. The word has two uses. Since the late seventeenth century it has become an essential concept of mathematics, applicable only to things which consist of numerable parts and meaning 'having no limit or end, real or assigned' (*O.E.D.*). Thus a line or surface may be considered as extending indefinitely, without limit and not returning into itself at any finite distance. But when the idea of infinity is applied, say, to knowledge, power, beauty, goodness, etc., it is better to use the words 'perfect', 'perfection', or 'complete'. For it is the awareness of the possibility of such perfection which inspires both the scientist and the artist. Without such belief, the comprehension of a mystery to be understood would wane and the 'drive' of many scientists and philosophers would sooner or later be extinguished. This is the faith that many live by and the mainspring of their joy and dedication.

Values as the expression of the central order
Many process philosophers are of the conviction that their studies eventually bring them to the point at which some form of theism is seen to be inevitable. This is a viewpoint which I share; for surely the belief in an all-encompassing process, purpose, or design must inevitably be theistic.

We may fittingly conclude by briefly discussing the views of one of the most outstanding of contemporary physicists, who supports and extends the view of Pasteur (see Chapter 4) that the ideals behind both the arts and the sciences are reflections from the 'infinite'. Werner Heisenberg (1971) says,

> The problem of values is nothing but the problem of our acts, goals and morals. It concerns the compass by which we must steer our ship if we are to set a true course through life. The compass itself has been given different names by various religions and philosophies . . . but I have a clear impression that all such formulations try to express man's relatedness to a central order. In the final analysis the central order, or the 'One' as it used to be called with which we commune in the language of religion, must win out. . . .
> If we ask Western man what is good, what is worth striving for and what has to be rejected, we shall find time and again, that his answers reflect the ethical norms of Christianity even when he has long since lost all touch with Christian images and parables. If the magnetic

force which has guided this particular compass—and what else was its source but the central order ?—should ever become extinguished, terrible things may happen to mankind, far more terrible even than concentration camps and atom bombs.

I believe Heisenberg to be entirely right over this. But of course, however supreme and perfect we may feel the Western insights that have stemmed from the Christian revelation to be, we must never forget that such a conclusion must on no account be attributed solely to this source. It is essential, and also very encouraging, to remain always aware that even a number of those indigenous religions which have been displaced and often scorned by the advance of Christian civilization both in Africa and in the New World, contain the germs of beliefs having close similarity to some of the major tenets of Christianity. Thus R. R. Marett in his distinguished book *Faith, hope and charity in primitive religion* (1932) has much of high importance to say on this matter. (See also Hardy, 1975, Ch. 5.)

But to me one of the clearest and most beautiful examples of this comes from the Amerindian tribe of the Shawnees, who were dispossessed of their Oklahoma lands in 1839. John Collier (1947) tells how force was seldom employed to secure good conduct; rather each person was his own judge. Deceitfulness was a crime, and absolute honesty towards each other the basis of character. This wonderfully contented and coherent society was achieved by the inculcation of two basic rules:

1. Do not kill or injure your neighbour, for it is not him that you injure, you injure yourself.
2. Do not wrong or hate your neighbour, for it is not him that you wrong, you wrong yourself. Moneto, the Supreme Being, loves him also as she loves you.

This inspired tribal ethic supported the sundered bands of the Shawnees, intact and in good heart, for more than half a century until they were once more reunited. And in the Pueblo cultures of Taos, beliefs were expressed in impressive rituals of great aesthetic worth. Truly contemplation of some of these rich cultures, which were many and diverse, should make us feel utterly humble.

References to Chapter 5

Agar, W. E. (1943) *The theory of the living organism*, Melbourne University Press, Melbourne.

Birch, C. (1974) 'Chance, necessity and purpose' in *Studies in the philosophy of biology* (eds. F. J. Ayala and T. Dobzhansky), Macmillan, London.

Collier, J. (1947) *Indians of the Americas*, Norton, New York.

Grene, M. (1966) *The knower and the known*, Faber and Faber, London.

Heisenberg, W. (1971) *Physics and beyond: encounters and conversations*, George Allen and Unwin, London.

Lewontin, R. C. (1974) *The genetic basis of evolutionary change*, Columbia University Press, New York and London.

Marett, R. R. (1932) *Faith, hope and charity in primitive religion*, Clarendon Press, Oxford.

Overman, R. H. (1976) ' "Life", "Purpose" and "the Inheritance of Acquired Characteristics" ' in Cobb and Griffin (1977): see below.

Popper, K. (1976) *Unended quest: an intellectual autobiography*, Fontana-Collins, London. (See especially pp. 180–96 and associated references.)

Price, H. H. (1932) *Perception*, Methuen, London.

Skinner, B. F. (1971) *Beyond freedom and dignity*, Knopf, New York and Jonathan Cape, London.

Whitehead, A. N. (1926) *Science and the world*, Cambridge University Press, Cambridge, and Macmillan, New York.

—— —— (1929) *Process and reality: an essay in cosmology*, Cambridge University Press, Cambridge, and Macmillan, New York.

For those who wish to begin a deeper study of Whitehead and the modern interpretation of his work, the following are recommended:

Bruner, J. S. (1974) *Beyond the information given*, Allen and Unwin, London.

Burgers, J. M. (1965) *Experience and conceptual activity*, M.I.T. Press, Cambridge, Mass.

—— —— (1975) 'Causality and anticipation, *Science* **189**, 194–8.

Cobb, J. B. (1965) *A Christian natural theology: based on the thought of Alfred North Whitehead*, Westminster Press, Philadelphia.

—— —— and Griffin, David Ray (eds.) (1977) *Mind in nature: essays on the interface of science and philosophy*, University Press of America, Washington, D.C.

Cousins, E. H. (ed.) (1972) *Hope and the future of man*, Garnstone Press, London.

—— —— (ed.) (1972) *Process theology: basic writings*, Newman Press, New York.

Emmet, D. (1966) *Whitehead's Philosophy of Organism*, 2nd edn., Macmillan, London, and St. Martin's Press, New York. (See especially new Preface, pp. xi–xliii.)

Gregory, R. L. (1974) *The concepts and mechanism of perception*, Duckworth, London.

Hardy, Alister (1975) *The biology of God*, Cape, London. (See especially Chs. 5, 10, and 11.)

Lawrence, N. (1974) *Alfred North Whitehead: a primer of his philosophy*. Twayne Publishers Inc., New York.

Reese, W. L., and Freeman, E. (eds.) (1964) *Process and divinity*, Open Court, La Salle, Illinois.

Sherburne, D. W. (1966) *A key to Whitehead's process and reality*, Collier-Macmillan, London, and Macmillan, New York.

Waddington, C. H. (1975) 'The New Atlantis revisited', Royal Society Bernal Lecture, 1975, *Proc. Roy. Soc. Ser. B*, Vol. 190, 301–14.

Index